I am not a black man

I am a man who is black

John Edgecombe

BROKEN
JUSTICE

BLACK SCANDAL

THE REAL REASON I SHOT THE GUN.

First published 2002 © John Edgecombe

The right of John Edgecombe to be identified as Author
of this work has been asserted by him in accordance with
the copyright, Designs and Patents Act. 1988.

Published by Westworld International Limited.
London England.
020 8788 2455

westworldinternational.com

A CIP catalogue record for this book is available from
the British Library. ISBN 0-952-9215-6-1

Printed and bound by Mackays of Chatham, Kent.
Cover designed by Tiger Designs.
Distributed by Central Books 020 8986 4854

ME AND MY GUN

CONTENTS

INTRODUCTION

My name is John Edgcombe. I fired the gun that opened the whole John Profumo/Christine Keeler Scandal. Much has been written about why I pulled the trigger but now here is the truth – my story.

Who was involved? The most powerful top government officials and organised crime bosses enforced it all. At least they tried to!

Christine Keeler introduced me to a mind-blowing scene with top ministers involved in wild sex orgies. The outrageous parties were so explicit they would have made any Hollywood film seem boring.

Politicians high up in power were plotting against each other and changing sides so quickly nobody knew what was going on.

I thought governments were run on issues such as health and education. I never dreamt that taxpayers' money was actually used to investigate the opposition's sex orgies from the night before.

Why have I never spoken before?

Read my story and you will understand that I really was the black pawn being check-mated by the all-powerful white Kings and Queens of society.

Part of what happens to us all in life is dictated by fate and my fate was obviously meeting that gorgeous chick,

Christine Keeler. I fell so deeply in love with her I just couldn't get out of the political arena.

How much did drugs play a role in it all?

The key players all went to bed with Keeler: it was because of her that Lucky Gordon got cut, the bullets got fired, Profumo resigned and so much more. If Keeler hadn't smoked so much dope would the whole show have played out differently?

The early 60's were a liberation period. We were the first generation that was growing up without a war. There was money to spend. Fashion was changing. We had our own music and as teenagers we weren't being sent of to join another army.

Corruption comes at the highest possible levels and as that jigsaw in its madness slotted together what I witnessed was beyond all possible belief.

Sex? People haven't changed and our thoughts and desires are the same forty years on.

Is there a lesson for the ministers today?

Perhaps my story has the answers!

THE BEAUTIFUL CHRISTINE KEELER

CHAPTER 1
IN THE BEGINNING

The Profumo/Keeler scandal. What really happened?

How did the Harold Macmillan Government fall?

How did the War Lord Jack Profumo get trapped into giving away the country's secrets?

How did the East End Gangsters, the infamous Kray Twins, help Harold Wilson bring the Labour Government to power?

Sex orgies with top Government Officials, drug parties, and murder. The Christine Keeler/Profumo affair in 1962 monopolised the front pages all over Europe.

It was my trial and conviction for attempted murder, that led to the whole can of worms exploding. Profumo resigned. Vassal, the Russian Agent, disappeared, Stephen Ward was murdered and the Labour government got into power.

What part did the Russians, the Germans, and MI5 play in it all? Who was actually behind these mysteries and who was the real benefactor?

I am now an old man and after living with my secrets for over forty years, I feel ready to reveal all.

Why am I telling my story?

I am telling it as it was to try to even the scales of justice!

Like myself then, the black minority and poor now are still being exploited all over the world, so the 'fat cats' in their respectable government/public positions can have what they want. All countries have two sets of laws; one for the masses, and one for the chosen few, and that's how it was in the summer of 1962.

It all started one afternoon when, stoned out of my head, I was on my way to score some dope in Bayswater. It was then that I met the other major pawn in that political game, an eighteen-year-old girl from Redhill, Christine Keeler.

The sun was beating down, and as I took a big drag from my giant spliff, someone called out to me from a black cab. It was Paula Hamilton-Marshall, a high-class hostess whose lifestyle was close to that of royalty. There in the back of the cab sat Paula, looking very elegant in her fitted cream suit. Next to her sat a beautiful young dark-haired girl, who glared at me with large seductive eyes. This girl was lying backwards practically hiding. She looked terrified. Her expression triggered off my early warning system. I went on red alert. Her name was Christine Keeler and over the next twelve weeks, between us, we would change the course of political history. I joined the girls in the cab and we soon arrived at Paula's flat in Devonshire Street, a very fashionable part of central London.

There at the entrance stood a sinister looking black guy. "It's him. It's him," whispered Christine as she lowered her head. At that time she was actually hiding from a vicious black thug called Lucky Gordon. Some time before, Lucky had kidnapped Christine and armed with a hatchet, held her prisoner in his flat for two days.

Fortunately, it was not Lucky Gordon. It was just a guy standing in the doorway, so we all went into Paula's flat. Pete, a friend of ours, arrived a short while later, and when he rang the bell, Christine almost jumped out of her skin. She was so wired-up she had already bitten off all her nails. Pete had some hash with him, but upstairs in the flat we soon discovered that he had been ripped off. The smoke he had bought was no good. The three of them decided to head to Christine's new hideaway where she was having a flat warming party. I saw this as my opportunity to get out and leave them all, so I suggested I take my own cab, pick up some dope, and join them all at Sheffield Terrace later. Christine said, "Money's no problem. We will all take one cab, first to Battersea to pick up your dope, then head on to my new flat." Moments later we were all huddled together in another cab. It was then that a strange feeling came over me. To this day I remember it all so clearly. I had a premonition that something bad was going to happen and later, for sure, it did. I had a pang of nerves and a sudden eagerness to escape, but at the same time I felt compelled to stay. There I was in the back of a London cab floating along on a cloud of hash, unaware of the world I was getting sucked into: a world full of violence and sinister encounters. It was my destiny, written in the scrolls of Johnny Edgecombe.

Christine was petrified of Lucky since her recent horrific ordeal with him. She had already been into the Chelsea police station, where she reported the incident, but

Lucky's four brothers made some serious threats to her, so Christine was forced to drop all charges.

In the 1960s, London was run by fear in both the black and white communities. In the white sector were the Kray twins, whose aspiration to become international gangsters was about to be realised. In those next twelve weeks the Krays were to come uninvited into the middle of my own world.

The cab soon arrived at Sheffield Terrace where a sex and drugs party began. Some time later, in the early hours of the morning, the party mellowed and I found myself alone with Christine.

"I am going to split," I said.

To which she replied, "Do you have to go?"

I said, "No I don't have to go, but you guys are trying to get me involved in some shit. So why don't you tell me who you're afraid of?"

Christine then told me the whole story about Lucky Gordon. I was surprised, I knew Lucky Gordon and asked Christine how the hell she had got involved with him. She told me all the messy details. I just sat back and listened. Profumo, Stephen Ward. I just took it all with a pinch of salt. I was unimpressed by the story but totally captivated by Christine. It was all happening quickly but I was falling deeply in love with this young beauty. From that moment on the sex was indescribable. Christine and I could certainly reach the heights of pure ecstasy and after that evening of passion I stayed for the next eight weeks.

We seemed always to be in bed and when we weren't making love, we would spend hours talking. Christine began to talk deeply about her life, which by that time was totally out of control. I didn't realise, as we lay talking and smoking, that the characters involved would soon become a major part of my life. Looking back it was like some sordid soap opera being played out in real life, of which I had just joined the cast.

The cast already in that soap were:

John Profumo.	War Minister
Valerie Hudson	Profumo's Wife
Mandy Rice Davies	Hostess
Harold Macmillan	Prime Minister
Dr Stephen Ward	Osteopath
Peter Rachman	Racketeer/Landlord
Lucky Gordon	Jamaican Thug
Eugene Ivanov	Russian Officer
Lord Astor	Aristocrat
Emil Savundra	Wealthy Indian Fraudster
President Kennedy	President of United States

Cast appearing in next episode were:

Johnny Edgecombe	Myself
Ronald Kray	East End Gangster
Reginald Kray	East End Gangster
Harold Wilson	Leader of the Opposition Party
Barbara Castle	Shadow Minister
Ed Wayne	American Secret Service Agent

I had never shot a gun before and when I look back it all seems like a bad dream, from which I awoke much later during my long prison sentence.

Up until then I was just a good time hustler, but that was all about to change.

I could never have dreamt what was to be as I left my home, a small Caribbean sun filled island, all those years ago. I was just fifteen years old when with only a few small possessions I arrived in England.

SCANDAL THE MAIN PLAYERS

CHRISTINE KEELER & STEPHEN WARD

JOHN PROFUMO & LORD DENNING

THE KRAY TWINS & HAROLD WILSON

HAROLD MACMILLAN & EUGENE IVANOV

CHAPTER 2
GROWING UP IN THE CARIBBEAN

I was born on the small island of Antigua in 1932. Antigua is a heavenly place with fifty-two beaches, one for each week of the year. Antigua is drenched in history. Lord Nelson had his own private dockyard there to service his ships as they sailed round the world. I grew up in the St. Johns district called 'Fibree'.

Our house was a fixed house, which meant it couldn't be moved like other mobile homes, which were common on the Island. I was the last of eight brothers and sisters that I am aware of. I say that because my father was a sailor, and as the saying goes, 'a girl in every port' was not far from the truth. My mum and Dad had an odd relationship. Although my mum was constantly uptight over Dad's other women, his unfaithfulness was never mentioned. It was just somehow accepted. My mum, however, always quietly interrogated me every time my father took me on one of his sea ventures. Dad's boat, a schooner, transported drums of gasoline for the 'Esso' company from Trinidad to Antigua. When I was about three years old my father took me away to Barbados without permission. My mum, however, very swiftly sailed over to rescue me.

As I grew older, going off to sea with Dad became a major part of my childhood.

My father was quite the local hero. He was known in every port as 'Captain Johnny'. Dad's boat,

'Perseverance', was about one hundred feet long and usually was overloaded with gasoline drums. On many occasions we found ourselves on rough seas, where we would have to manually pump out water to stop the boat sinking. When we visited Trinidad, Dad would often leave me in a bar called 'Higgins' whilst he did his business. After a long wait, we would usually visit 'Bidy', his local girl. She, like most of Dad's girlfriends, was extremely kind to me, feeding me up with one of her great feasts and telling me lots of amusing stories. As a young boy it was like having a dozen mothers.

Once, during a really bad storm at sea, we lost our sails and had to stop in Granada. Two of our headsails were broken, so we had to stay in the port to make the repairs. My Dad got hopelessly drunk with one of his local women and was in no condition to skull our longboat back to the schooner, which was reared about half a mile out at sea. As a six year old I had to get us both back on board. In quite rough seas, without help from Dad who was still swigging his rum, I somehow got the longboat alongside our main boat. How Dad, still holding the bottle of rum, climbed up the rope ladder into the boat, was a miracle. But he did and subsequently passed out. The next morning he regained consciousness and we sailed on to Antigua. For a six-year-old this was no picnic and the next day my hands were covered with blisters.

At a very young age I learned to swim. Dad used to throw me into the sea with a rope tied around my chest under my arms. He tightened the rope with a bowling knot. From that time onwards you couldn't keep me out of the water. I was a human fish.

Back home in Antigua I played with toy sailing boats, spending hours sailing the tiny things from one end of the bay to another. It was great fun.

As a family we were classed as a respectable one, therefore as kids we had to wear shoes. The waterfront kids just went everywhere bare foot. As a child I did not like wearing shoes, and each day as soon as I was out of my mother's sight, I would take them off and hang them around my neck.

One day, when I should have been at school, I met a friend of my brother, 'Sonny'. I asked him, if he wanted to go sailing. We borrowed a boat without consent and sailed around for two hours. When we arrived back at the jetty, I could see the owner with the police, so I quickly took the boat back to its moorings. I left Sonny in the boat, tied my clothes on my head, and swam home. I had a quick wash in the local public showers, got dressed, and feeling very pleased with my clean getaway, went indoors. As I entered the yard, my mother took one look at my feet and screamed;

"Where are your shoes?"

I looked down at my bare feet. In my haste I had left my sneakers on board. I had to tell my mother the whole story. She then marched me back to the harbour, where we got my shoes back.

When I was ten-years-old, the war in Europe was in full swing and with no advance warning whatsoever, my Dad became an American citizen and left us all. I was not to see him again for twenty years. He just sold his boat and disappeared out of our lives. Dad had always been my hero and as a ten-year-old, it all upset me a great deal.

A short while later, Mum allowed me to go to Trinidad, for five weeks during my mid-summer school break, to visit my Uncle Piper. The purpose of the trip was to help me to get over my father's sudden disappearance. I stayed with my uncle for about four weeks and then ran away from him to live on the streets. I spent my time hanging round the docks, sleeping in stray boats. I was a good hustler and knew how to ask for food in Spanish and often got given food and shelter. After six months of living on the waterfronts, I hitchhiked lifts on various boats in order to get back to my mother in Antigua.

On my first boat ride home I fell asleep in the foxal, which is a portion within the bow at the front of the ship. When you sail out of Trinidad you go through a pass called the "Bocas". The Bocas pass divides Venezuela from Trinidad. This pass can be very rough and I awoke to find we had lost a mast and were in severe danger of sinking.

Miraculously we made it to the Island of St. Lucia, and at the dockside, very shaken up, most of the crew quit and left the boat refusing to sail on. Fortunately, on St Lucia, my older sister's husband had rented a house for her, which she had never moved into and had been left unoccupied. Breaking into that empty building was easy, and a comfortable night's sleep inside was much appreciated.

I stayed there for a while and later I met a boy called Aki. By the house was a breadfruit tree, and I gave him permission to pick some fruit. A woman neighbour, who claimed she owned the tree, went berserk and started screaming. She performed "voodoo" on me and chanted some kind of curse.

A day or so later I got a job as a deck boy on a ship called 'Ipana,' which was going to another island. I was on board getting to know the boat when suddenly I started shivering. In that hot Caribbean weather I knew something was radically wrong. Freezing cold, I left the boat, went back to the house and lay on the bed. The electricity in the house was not working, but as I lay there unable to get up, the lights started to flicker.   I was petrified.

This living nightmare continued for several days until a girl living locally became my nurse. She gave me 'Sapentea' by boiling up a root. The drink made me sweat a great deal but the sweating led to me being cured.

About three weeks later another boat came to the Island and some of the people on board knew my dad and also my grandfather, whom I had never met. I was very excited when they told me they were sailing to 'St. Thomas,' where this old man lived.

My great grandfather was a white Irish man who had served as a second in command sailor on a boat. The captain of that boat couldn't write, so my great grandfather had apparently signed an important document for him. Instead of signing the captain's name, which he should have done, my great grandfather signed his own, and as a result, ended up marrying some aristocratic woman in Dominica.

His son, my grandfather, was also white and lived in a large house, in a very affluent part of the Island. The old boy was very pleased to see me. He was now around eighty years old and stood shaking. This frail old man was far from the image I had always had in mind of my grandfather. During my stay there he cared for me well and I ate like a king. Soon after I had gained all my strength back I was put back on a boat for Antigua, where, at home, I found my mother cooking.

"Hi mum, what's for dinner?" I asked sheepishly.

"Where on earth have you been boy?" my mother yelled. "Nobody knew where you were. You've been missing for six months, and here you are acting as if nothing has happened, as if I'd just sent you to the shops."

"Sorry," I cried, holding my hands in the air.

Somehow my mother had known that I had been ill. She had received a spiritual message from her late mother. My mother was gifted in that way. She called it messages from the other side.

On one occasion, my brother Papasido stole some money from my mother. My mother discovered the loss and went absolutely mad. She made all her children sit around the kitchen table, then placed a pair of scissors in between the pages of a bible and tied the book with string. Then, one by one, she held the Bible by the string with each of us and repeated the following prayer, "By St Peter, by St Paul, by the living God that made us all. Emily took the money." She repeated this chant three times with each child's name and if the Bible stayed still she would move onto the next. When it got to Papasido's turn the Bible spun-off completely. Papasido froze. At first Papisodo said nothing, but eventually he broke down and confessed. My mother, although annoyed and extremely hurt, eventually forgave him.

Over the following months, I got bored and decided to go back to school. One day, in school, my brother-in-law came to me with exciting news.

The next chapter of my life was about to emerge and what a chapter it was to be.

CHAPTER 3
LEAVING ANTIGUA

My brother-in-law was the local harbour master, and had come to tell me about a young sailor. The sailor was working as a pantry boy aboard a big Harrison ship called 'HMS Prospector'. The boy had been taken very ill and the ship was about to sail.

"They need a new pantry boy and you can have the job," he explained.

This ship, carrying sacks of sugar for the big sugar company, 'Tate and Lyle', was going to an island many thousands of miles away. The island was called England. Due to sail in two hours, this left me little time, so I rushed home to tell my mother the news. My mother, who knew where the ship was heading, was horrified.

"How can I let my baby go half way across the world?" she cried. I first got my brother-in-law, to argue my case, but soon all my brothers and sisters had joined in on my behalf. My mother, who was still against me going, warned them all,

"If I let him go, we won't see him again."

But there was no stopping me. "I'm going some time with or without your blessing," I cried out.

She just stared at me and didn't say a word. At just fifteen I had a strong mind and there was no way I would be persuaded otherwise. Eventually my mother gave half a smile and nodded. She hurried me down to Dr Winters, the family doctor, to obtain a health certificate.

Officially, the Captain shouldn't have allowed me to sail without union papers, but they were desperate for a pantry boy so he accepted my local doctor's certificate. My brother-in-law took me in his boat to get aboard the main ship, which was about half a mile out at sea. As we left, I turned round and saw my mother, and my brothers and sisters waving from the harbour. As our small boat approached the ship, they gradually faded away. "Goodbye," I whispered. Arriving alongside the big ship I climbed aboard. There I was, standing on the stern of the boat, watching the Isle of Antigua vanish into the distance.

All my worldly possessions were in a paper bag: two pairs of socks, some T-shirts, and some underpants. Feeling alone I had a moment of apprehension, and considered swimming ashore, but we were too far out and I knew it was impossible. I was now heading towards a new life. If only then I had known what was in store. Standing on the deck I took a deep breath, realising that this was the time when I had to stop being a boy and become a man. My first step was to report to the ship's officer, which I promptly did.

This was my first experience on a steamboat. I called it a 'tramp' ship, which, translated, means an old ship. It was a typical British ship with typical British standards, those in the top decks and those at the bottom. The officers and the sailors were all white, while the trimmers, stokers, and cooks were all black. In total, there were about thirty passengers: ten white officers and twenty black crewmen.

I had never before imagined that one day I would be sailing to England. I was just a kid of fifteen, who had excitedly agreed to this adventure, without really giving the idea any thought.

Here I was, working on board this huge steam ship and heading towards the unknown. The only taste of British culture I had had, was that of the English sailors visiting Antigua. We, locals, had a nickname for the British sailors. We called them "Limeys". They were always broke to the extent that our local hookers wouldn't even consider their desperately low cash offers for sex. The only time our hookers came out was for the visiting American ships.

Fifty-five years ago England controlled much of the world, so my perception of England was a land of almighty power. Here I stood, looking out on clear blue waters, wondering how great this powerful land would be.

My job as pantry boy was to serve the white officers their meals, which were always so lavish. I worked hard in that pantry and was ordered about like a slave by the older workers. The officers were quite civil towards me, but I knew my place, and that was below deck, far away from the luxurious surroundings that the officers enjoyed.

The two weeks soon flew by and finally we were approaching the Liverpool Docks, in the north of

England. With my eyes, wide open, I stared towards what seemed like a million lights, illuminating the distant land.

There I stood, with my few possessions, excited that soon my feet would be standing on this land of lights. The ship I had come over on would return to Antigua at the end of that week, so this gave me a chance to explore my new surroundings and perhaps look for another boat to sail on elsewhere.

Those few days on land soon passed and that was when I was to discover the greatest shock of my life. I was now told that I could not join another ship unless I was a member of the pool. It was all very complicated for a fifteen-year-old to understand. It had something to do with the ship's union. No union card, no sailing. So therefore I went to join the Union, which stated,

"Get the sailing job, join the ship first, and then you can join the union."

I went back to join the ship, but the boson repeated,

"I cannot employ you without your union card."

Here I was, a young black boy, fifteen-years-old, in a very strange land. No job, no union, no passport, and most importantly no home. All I had was my medical certificate.

Fortunately, a fellow member of the crew, called Cecil, actually lived in Liverpool. Like a saviour from above, he temporarily rescued me from my nightmare. He offered me a roof over my head and at least a so-called start.

During those first couple of weeks in Liverpool, I was exposed to adult life and its racial problems, catapulted from the innocence of Antigua to adulthood in the ghetto of Liverpool. It was all new and very challenging.

In 1949 blacks and whites in Liverpool were very much divided and there was a lot of conflict going on. Most black people then were either African or Jamaican. The Jamaicans did not trust the Africans because the Africans had a culture and a language of their own. The Africans also had different dialects depending on which part of Africa they came from. The Jamaicans on the other hand, had no proper language of their own. The British, during their colonisation, had robbed the Jamaicans of their culture, leaving them with a broken language and a chip on their shoulder. Race was a major problem in those days. The worst hit were the half-castes, an enemy of both the blacks and the whites.

After the war, the UK Government had advertised in Jamaica and British Guyana for black men to come over and work on the railways. Many black men had come over, only to find the work very hard and the pay exceptionally low. It wasn't long before these new immigrants got tired of the early starts and bored with the mundane work. This soon led to them looking for an escape, for an easier life, one that was more in line with the dope smoking lifestyle of back home. Lurking in the back streets of Liverpool this easier way was just waiting to be discovered.

At that time, living off immoral earnings carried a maximum sentence of only three months imprisonment. So, to some blacks destined for a career on the railways for £6 a week, this was a much brighter prospect. We came from the bright sunshine so working on the railways in the pouring rain, and living in a small room, with a lino floor, was not so appealing. The most important things to us young black men were; pussy, which meant having a girl to have sex with, and having somewhere to live. A black man would go to the black man's clubs, where the hookers would hang out along with other easy-going girls, who were potential hookers. Seeing all this easy money was an eye opener. The chance to earn some serious cash by just putting one or two girls out on the game seemed an opportunity too good to miss.

I am genuinely not trying to make excuses, but the black population had a lot of hurdles to jump. Racism was everywhere. Notice Boards advertising rooms to let were clearly labelled with, "No Blacks Please". It was due to this continued racism and lack of realistic opportunities, which led to some blacks getting involved with the red light district. Prostitution was big business; it offered a chance to some to live a far more comfortable and prosperous life. Some black men, who were originally hardworking nine-to-fivers, took the easy way out and who can blame them?

After several attempts of trying to obtain the correct union papers, I realised that it was a total waste of time. It was an impossible situation, a real catch 22. Cecil, the man who had put a roof over my head, suggested that I go to Tiger Bay in Cardiff, where I could probably board a Panamanian Ship. These ships were far more relaxed in their checking procedures and would be far easier for me to board. There was every chance, Cecil explained, that I could get a working passage without the required papers.

A day or so later, I was on a train heading towards Cardiff. With the very last of my borrowed money, I hid in the train's toilet to dodge my fare. When we arrived I leapt from a window and ran towards a trolley bus, which would take me to Tiger Bay.

CHAPTER 4
TIGER BAY

Tiger Bay was somehow kinder to black people. That was perhaps because the population of blacks was greater. Night and day there were numerous ships coming in and out. There were lots of 'missions' where the sailors would stay while they were in town. Down at the docks it was like a melting pot, with all different nationalities and mixed colours blending into each other. It was the only place in the UK, at that time, where a black man felt safe far, far, safer than Liverpool.

In those rows of tiny terraced houses were: Maltese, Arabs, Somalies, Africans and West Indians all living together.

Tiger Bay had an enormous wall, which ran from Bute Street all the way down to the Docks. Running off the main road all the streets looked the same. I was now just sixteen years old and like any young man would, I found it all very exciting.

By now, I no longer had any contact with my mother. I was too busy growing up real fast. There was gambling in the streets, drugs, and prostitution – in front of my eyes it was all going on.

In order to get social security and a blue ration book I lied, saying that I was eighteen. It was 1950 and there were still big shortages after the war. Sweets, sugar and butter were hard to come by and this encouraged an illegal market, with the arriving sailors selling smuggled goods on the side.

Ghetto areas always bring four vital ingredients; crime, drugs, prostitution and gambling. Whichever country you were in, you always found the same. In the bigger towns, the gambling brought about seedy casino type clubs, whereas in Tiger Bay there were no clubs. Instead, all this gambling took place outside in the street. Gambling was illegal, so every game had its lookout man watching for the police. There were small games for six pence. Then there were the big-time games for up to £5, where the sailors, just off ship, with their pockets bulging, could lose all their wages. This often caused fights so bloodstains on the pavements where the game had taken place were common.

The police-lookout-man would shout, "Heads up!" when he saw the men in blue approaching. With the game in progress, the guy actually rolling the dice at the time would try to stand up quickly and hide the money. The police always interrupted things just at the wrong time, and on numerous occasions, in all the turmoil, an opportunist thief would grab the money and run. This was a risky thing to do, because getting caught meant a severe beating.

Tiger Bay was fascinating, and to me, as a teenager, it was a new world exploding on every street corner. Joe Erskin, the boxer, fought Henry Cooper for the British title while I lived in Tiger Bay. We often saw Joe running as part of his training. Joe's dad was one of the leading illegal bookmakers that took bets in the street on horse races.

At sixteen years old I was a tall boy and probably looked older, but really I was still only a kid, a long, long, way from home.

While I was still sleeping in the Seamen's Missions I met Miss Beetie. She was an old white woman of about sixty and somehow we got talking one day whilst I was queuing up to get my social payment. She offered me a room in her house, which was far more comfortable than the Seamen's Mission. She was a funny old lady who told me stories about the old days. She became like the mother I no longer had, and also taught me how to cook rice, which helped the little money I had go further.

During that time, I met the Freemans who became like a surrogate family. The father was from Jamaica and had three daughters and a son called Johnny. I never actually lived with them, but always popped in to eat, or just hang around. I also left some of my clothes at their house. For me, a young kid in the wilderness of a strange country, it was my safe base. The daughters all went out with the GI's, so there always seemed to be plenty of everything about.

There were many weird and wonderful characters around the bay, one of which was called Rolled Gold. He lived on his own in Lowden Square, and each week when he got his dole money, he would cook an enormous meal, which somehow actually lasted for three days: Friday, Saturday, and Sunday! For these three days, stoned out of his mind on dope, he would stand outside his house for half an hour at a time blowing his saxophone full blast. You could hear his music streets away. As the dope high wore off, he would go back inside for another puff on his joint. He never ever spoke to anyone.

His private saxophone party would go on all weekend until the food and hash ran out during the early hours of Monday morning. Then, he would simply go back to sleep, non-stop all through the day and night, until it was time to get up again the following Friday. Then he would collect a new week's dole money, buy his dope and food, and his long weekend party would start all over again. During the week nobody saw or heard of him behind those closed doors.

Another oddball was the Indian restaurant owner called Babba. Babba was a short 'roly-poly' Indian man, who desperately tried to run a tight ship in his little curry house. Often, people would eat the meal and simply do a runner without paying, so he would stand by the door to stop these non-payers. It was funny to watch because when Baba had to go to the kitchen or the toilet, there was another mad exodus of non-paying customers.

My first smoke of dope was in a room in Bute Street, near the mission I was living in. I don't think I was actually supposed to smoke that day. It just kind of happened.

I was with these three guys, all about four years older than me. They were sitting in a circle passing round a joint. The first few times the joint went round it missed me altogether, but about the third or forth time it passed round, the joint was handed to me.

I took my first puff on my very first joint.

After we had finished smoking we went out to play billiards. Down at the corner the rush hit me I felt like I was walking on air. It was very strange. I went back to the room and flopped out on a bed but the bed suddenly took off, twisting around the room. At one stage the bed twisted and turned so hard that it threw me off and I fell on the floor. The floor now took off with me on it. With the floor flying through the sky I gave up and swore I would never smoke dope again. That oath was ignored. Here I am 50 years later a real dope head.

Within days I had a full time job smoking dope.

Dope smoking then, was like a religious thing of sorts. The Jamaicans had a ritual when they smoked a Chilham Pipe. You had to pass the pipe to the right and if you made a mistake and passed it to the left you had to pay a forfeit and buy the next bag of smoke.

This was 1950 and smoking dope was quite a rare thing. It had only just arrived from the other side of the world. At that time, there were only about twelve people in the whole of Tiger Bay who actually smoked dope, and we were regarded as the outcasts. We twelve became our own private society. In those days people didn't understand about hash or what to expect a person to behave like if they smoked a spliff. Everybody knew what to expect from a drunk, but a spliff was a mystery associated with that weird jazz music the blacks played.

Jazz was the devil's music. Jazz and dope went together.

In the early fifties there were no dope dealers as such. If you wanted dope you just had to ask one of the seaman who had just come in on a coaster from Africa. The price of dope was then about two shillings per kilo.

Those days, the sailors could bring back a pillowcase full of dope, because the boarder check in Tiger Bay was non-existent.

On some boats with Indian crews, you didn't even need money to get hash. With Indian sailors we used to swap second-hand suits and other stuff for some solid dope. Sometimes you would even get a curry to eat while still on board, thrown in on the deal!

There were five Jamaicans who originally all came over on a ship called 'Windrush' and they were the first pot-smoking Jamaicans to arrive on these shores.

We blacks were all poor in those days. We were economic slaves. Slavery hadn't finished, they had just changed the name to 'low pay and poverty', and I suppose the dope helped us cope.

And so were my teenage years in Tiger Bay, spending all day going around stoned, to everywhere and anywhere. There were fights, petty crime, and trouble on a daily basis, but somehow the funds always came in to buy more dope off the newly arrived ships. Dope-smokers drift together and those years floated by.

CHAPTER 5
STOW AWAY

Deep down I was a kid who just wanted to sail the world, but couldn't because I was unable to get on a ship. One day, a sailor who was getting off a boat, recognised me. He knew my Dad, and told me the address of my where he was living in New York. Now I knew exactly where my father was living in America, I decided to visit him.

Travel arrangements were simple.

I was simply going to stow away on a ship going to America. Looking back, I realize it was a dangerous thing to do, because in those days they still sometimes threw stowaways overboard.

Although my Dad was in New York, which is where I wanted to reach, when you travel as a stowaway you cannot dictate the town you travel to, you just have to hope that the boat is headed for the right country.

I arranged to stow away with a Jamaican guy called Red, who wanted to get back home. His idea was to get to America first and then somehow he would get a second boat over to Jamaica. Red was about seven years older than me, which gave me some courage, because even to me, as a cocky self-assured kid, stowing away to America was quite mind blowing.

Red and I arranged to meet down at the docks at midnight so we could sneak on board unnoticed. The boat was due to sail at first light. That night I waited and waited but Red never came. A couple of hours passed and not wanting to miss the chance, with my heart pumping, I thought, "Fuck it, I'm going alone."

I ran up the gangplank and looked for somewhere to hide. On deck, I saw a sailor coming towards me. He hadn't seen me and quickly I darted to the stern of the ship and climbed down the main hole. Deep, deep, down I went, and found myself on the ledge, by the propeller shaft. I had to lean backwards to stop falling on to the propeller and being sliced to death. After about an hour, there was an almighty noise, like a volcano and the whole world started to shake. It was the ship's engines starting. We were now sailing. I was so excited we were off to America. Clutching my paper bag containing a few apples for the trip, I was embarking on yet another adventure.

I waited a couple of hours until we were safely out at sea before climbing out to look for a safer, more comfortable place to spend the rest of that fourteen-day trip. I figured that now even if I was caught, I would still get to America, because we were too far out at sea to send me back to Tiger Bay.

It was very early in the morning and there was not a soul on deck as I made my way to the black sleeping quarters. There I found a locker room stuffed full of old tarpaulin. It was ideal, the perfect hiding place I thought, closing the door behind me, as I crawled underneath the tarpaulin. In the pitch black, I felt really quite safe, easing myself towards the back when suddenly I felt something warm, and that something was breathing.

I wasn't on my own. Here were two other stowaways, also getting a free ride. Soon we were all laughing because we knew each other from Tiger Bay. Both boys, Mark and Eric, were about five years older than me. They didn't have any food, so very quickly my apples disappeared. These boys somehow took charge and I was the one who was told to sneak out at night to steal food. Most nights I managed to take some of the bread and water that had been left out for the night-watch man, who must have been left feeling quite hungry. I knew the layout of the ship, so it was quite easy for me creeping about in the dark.

All went well for a few days, but then Eric got sick. He became very claustrophobic and started talking to himself all night. We both tried to calm him down, but he got worse and began sweating, so we decided that we had to give ourselves up.

We weren't that bothered, as we climbed up on deck, to find the Captain. We felt more like naughty schoolboys, which at sixteen years old, I still was really.

The Captain went off a bit, but he soon calmed down and decided that instead of locking us up, he would put us to work for the remainder of the trip. We were all given the same job, which was to chip the rust off the deck with a special little hammer called the chipping hammer.

On our knees, we had quite a laugh pretending our hammers were musical instruments, beating them in rhythm. Mark played bass with a very steady boom, boom, boom, while Eric and I were doing the faster lighter taps. We thought we were very musical with lots of talent, but the white head-cook who had to listen to the continual noise did not agree, so in a very rough voice he told us, "Shut the fuck up.

"You're not in the Jungle now." He went on and on.

Mark, who was even taller than me, wouldn't stand for all that shit and threw his hammer at the chef's chest. It winded him, and with one big punch, Mark floored him. From then on, no other sailors gave us any problems and we were left alone, with our hammers and the boom-boom music.

A few days later we arrived in Galveston, Texas.

"Well, here we are," I thought to myself, seeing the coast of America. "I'll soon be seeing my Dad." How wrong I was!

The ship's Captain had arranged a deal with the county jail to keep us locked up until they sailed off again. It was a safer bet for them, because while the ship was in port, if we had managed to escape into America, the shipping company would have had to pay a massive fine.

Although we were being locked up, in a funny way, the Captain was doing us a favour. Texas in those days was predominantly white, and a stray black man could easily have been shot. The county sheriff came on to the boat to collect us, and we all left very dramatically, like a scene from 'Amistad'. Led off, chained together in handcuffs, we were like black slaves going off to be sold. The three of us were bundled into the back of the Sheriff's car, a big station wagon, and driven off to the county jail.

The jail itself was a very frightening place. It was where the murderers and the rapists were kept before they went to court. We were taken inside and handed over to a guy called Joseph, a real tough cookie. Joseph began by demanding a three-dollar fine from each of us.

"Well," said Joseph. "If you're all skint, you must pay the fine by working."

We were given jobs. I was made the new county jail barber and now found myself cutting the hair of the most dangerous men in America. It was very nerve racking, and one day I accidentally cut someone's ear. The man was a killer, notorious in the area. He just stared at me, his eyes bulging, as we both watched in silence the blood trickle down the side of his face. I expected him to stand up and stab me with the scissors, but he just stared at me without saying a word.

One morning they brought in a black cowboy. It was the first time I even knew black cowboys existed. This guy was a giant of a man. His muscles were like mountains bulging through his shirt. When the cowboy arrived he wasn't tried in the Kangaroo Court like we had been. I asked Joseph why the cowboy himself was not tried.

Joseph smiled and went on to explain

Once a month the black cowboys came down from the hills, where they lived with their cattle and horses. They would hit town and get drunk, and smash up all the bars. The drunken cowboys were always caught, and just locked up for a night or so, never longer. The reason they were only locked up for a night was that the Sheriff knew that if they kept a black cowboy in the county jail for longer, the whole gang of cowboys, would soon come down from the hills and attack the jail, on mass.

We were in jail for quite some time, but the Sheriff didn't mind, he was getting well paid for it. Anyhow, time passed, and without cutting any more ears, I continued as the barber, until one morning the Sheriff told us it was time to leave.

Once again in chains, we were all driven back to the ship and soon we were out at sea, saying goodbye to America.

I never did get to see my Dad.

Back out at sea, the three of us were given our same jobs, and the musical hammers put out the beat without interruption, throughout the trip back to Europe.

A week or so later we were docking in North Germany. Here, there was no jail. It was 1950 and the Germans were still busy rebuilding the rubble from the war years. Not speaking German and being black, all three of us agreed that to go on the run in Germany would have been stupid. Without passports, we would have been caught very quickly.

CHAPTER 6
EARLY DAYS IN LONDON

Our boat left Germany and finally we docked in Northshields in the north of England. The three of us had no idea about what was to happen. We thought we were still going to get some pay, and were hanging around in our quarters when two immigration officers burst in. We were all arrested and taken to the local police station. The following morning we appeared in court and were charged with illegally stowing away on a ship. We were given twenty-eight days, which was the standard imprisonment for stowing away. From the courts, we were driven away to Durham Jail. At that time, I was seventeen years old and strictly speaking, I shouldn't have gone to an adult jail.

Apart from the jail in Texas, I had never been inside before, but prison was now an experience that was becoming a regular thing.

Twenty-eight days later we were all released, and found ourselves standing outside the jail, with hardly a penny between us.

We all walked to the nearest railway station and somehow managed, with only platform tickets, to sneak aboard several trains and hide without paying our fairs.

Eventually we arrived back in Cardiff and headed for Tiger Bay. The guys in Tiger Bay were surprised, but real glad to see us.

"Welcome back!" They cried out. "Tell us all about America!"

They held a special coming home celebration for us. The party included a large joint for each of us. This was the first time I had smoked hash since I had stowed away to go to America. The joint zapped me. I kept conscious, but just slumped back in my chair and drifted off into orbit. It was around this time that my adventurous mind began again to yearn for action, and the desire to move on to fresh pastures returned.

After a few weeks my life in Tiger Bay was once more becoming monotonous. The routine now became the same every day. We just woke up and got stoned. I really wanted to get on another boat and sail away to some far off land, but all that was about to change.

Two Jamaicans George and Dudley had recently arrived in Tiger Bay. They were about twenty-five and, for me as an eighteen-year-old, I was intrigued with these cool characters. George and Dudley talked about their adventures in London and it all seemed very exciting. They both dressed very sharply, in beige Burberry raincoats and expensive suits. I regularly smoked hash with these men and got to know them both well. These two guys were hardened hustlers and had come over with the first batch of Jamaicans in 1948. At this time there were probably only about a thousand black people in England, who were mainly Jamaicans.

A year later, in 1949, when I had come over, I was myself actually one of the first from the Lewood Islands.

One day, George and Dudley said they were going back to London and asked me if I would like to go with them. I agreed immediately. Arriving in London at Paddington Station, it seemed a vast place, and for me, a whole new life was opening up.

In London it was all happening, and after some difficulties, I found lodgings in Maida Vale. It was not easy to get digs because the anti-black attitude was so strong. When I walked the streets, or went in a café, I would be the only black person around, because in those days, there were so few of us in England.

The three of us had only been in London a short while, when I came up with the idea of me becoming an African Prince. I didn't actually want to become a Prince and live in Africa - the idea was very different.

The African Prince scam was quite simple and worked like this. I would go into an expensive jewellery shop, posing as a wealthy African Prince, and ask to see the engagement rings. I explained that the ring was for my fiancé, and kept repeating how much I was in love with her. The assistant would bring out a tray of rings and after looking them over I would say, "Haven't you got anything more expensive?" explaining that I only wanted the very best. On most occasions, the shop assistant would bring out another tray, containing much more expensive rings, leaving the first batch still out. It was at this point my two accomplices, standing in the street by the window, would enter the shop pretending they didn't know me. In the confusion of three customers being in the shop, one of them would steal a ring. As I continued to look at other rings, they would simply say, "We'll come back when you're not so busy." Then they would calmly leave the shop. We would all meet up later and George would sell the rings, or whatever we stole that day, to a dealer in the East End. I'm sure that George was actually getting paid more for each ring than what he said, but I was young and for me it was big money anyway. We got away with this for months, but as time went on, we were running out of jewellery shops in London. We decided to go further a field and finished up in Bristol. In an area called Templemead, we went into a jeweller's shop to operate the usual scam. This time our luck ran out. The assistant noticed a ring was missing and confronted me. I denied knowing the other two men and somehow got out of the shop. A few streets away, I found George and Dudley and warned them about the shop assistant. "He's going to call the police," I said. "We've got to split up now." George and Dudley wouldn't take any notice, and arrogantly insisted we all waited together at Bristol Station to catch the train back to London. I knew something was about to happen and very nervous I went to the station toilet to hide in a cubicle. All of a sudden I heard a policeman asking the station officer, if he had seen some black guys. The station officer replied, "Yes." After looking around the platform, the police came in to search the toilets. Here I was, trapped like a rabbit caught in the headlights, waiting for my cubical door to be opened.

After being tried in court, I was sentenced to a Young Persons Prison in Lewis for three months. In prison I was treated very badly. I was made to clean the toilets with a pumice stone, amongst other demeaning jobs. I was the only black person in that prison.

Three months later, I was discharged with a travel document and went back to Cardiff and Tiger Bay, where life continued on a cloud of hash.

It was around this time that I met a chick called Nelly, in a pub down by the docks. We started going out together and Nelly and I fell in love. Nelly had known for some time that I was going to London and was very enthusiastic to come with me. One day we just both packed our bags and with excitement left Tiger Bay.

Life in London, in those days, was impossible for a black man. We were pushed to the bottom of society's heap, with only the worst possible jobs and the lowest possible pay available. The main job available to black people was working at the bottom of the employment ladder on the railways.

There was no way I was going to slave for the railways, to be paid a pittance in wages for the rest of my life. That's how the future looked for a black man, fighting racism and being discriminated against, in England in the early sixties.

We were always discriminated against, not only in work, but in our social lives too. For a white woman to go out with a black man she would totally alienate herself from the rest of white society. She would get lots of stick, like being called 'nigger-lover,' by her neighbours. I'm not exaggerating. When Nelly and I went out for a drink together, we always got funny looks. On many occasions we were even refused service. Imagine what it's like to ask for a pint of beer only to be told, "No. We are not serving you." On every street corner there was graffiti on the walls, with anti black slogans like, 'Keep Britain White,' or 'Go home nigger!' For a black man to walk past these slogans every day was sickening. You knew you were not welcome. You felt like a leper, an outcast. To live like that was mental torture and many black guys ended up psychologically disturbed, living in psychiatric wards because they just couldn't deal with what was going on.

In the main, if it wasn't for the hookers, we black guys wouldn't have survived sexually, at all. White girls wouldn't go with black guys, because of fear of being ridiculed by other white people. During the late fifties, the government had only advertised for black men to come and work in England, not black women. By doing this, they had created a society of black, sexually frustrated, angry young men.

It was this discrimination that forced me, along with many others, to a live a life on the other side of the tracks. When I look back today, I regret some of the things I did. At least, I can honestly say I'm not so proud of them. But at that time, it seemed I had no choice and that society was pushing me into making my decisions.

Perhaps, if at the time, if I had been on trial with my conscience, the court case would have gone something like this:

Society:
"John, why don't you get a job on the railways, an honest job?"

John:

"Well, if I am going to do an honest job, I would like an honest wage."

Society:

"Well, we can't pay you any more!"

John:

"If you can't pay me any more, you can't afford to employ me. I go to work for me, not for you. There are other ways of making a living. Going to work for two pounds a week on the railways is not making a living. It is slavery! I go to work to support my family, not the railways."

Society:

"Well, what are you going to do then?"

John:

"Dope dealing, stealing, or put a chick on the game."

The cost of living in London was always extremely expensive and with dope prices so high, we had no choice. Now that I have three daughters of my own, I am not proud of what I did, but at the time it did not seem wrong.

It is fair to say that Nelly and I were extremely close when we originally met in Tiger Bay. Nelly was just a fun chick and like most of the girls in those days was quite free and easy.

After a while in London, Nelly and I had a chat about household economics, and as a couple, decided that she would go on the game, which meant becoming a prostitute. In those days, the wife, or girlfriend going on the game was a common practice and socially accepted amongst some black people. In many ways, it was no different from a couple, whose children were now at school, deciding that the wife's second income would boost finances. I know of many cases where a black man and a white chick, quite deeply in love, saved the deposit for their first home through the chick's immoral earnings. Other, more ambitious men, kept the chick at it to get the entire mortgage paid off early and a BMW in the drive. Whether it was conscience, or just the chick getting old, was a debatable point as to why this extra source of income would eventually dry up.

Having decided on Nelly's new profession, we started going to clubs, where all the other white girls were already established hookers. The chicks talked about the perks of being prostitutes, and soon Nelly was working the streets in Park Lane. We used meet up every night after Nelly had finished work, and go to one of the clubs. While Nelly was at work, I was out doing my own work, hustling dope.

The ghetto is not so pleasant and you can't be blamed for trying anything to avoid living there. Perhaps this is the reason why, fifty years later, street crime has surged and hard drug addiction has soared.

CHAPTER 7
SHEBEEN TIME

I was about twenty-two years old, when, in the early
fifties, I opened the very first Shebeen in London. A
Shebeen is a private residence where, with no licence,
you are open to the public to serve food and drinks while
they listened to jazz music. The Shebeen is like a secret
nightclub, similar to the 'Speak Easy's in America, in the
1930`s. I served an extra dish in my Shebeen, a very
special dish - dope.

My Shebeen was in Colville Terrace, Notting Hill Gate.
It was a flat on the first floor. When it was full, we had
about twenty to thirty people inside the flat. There was a
front room where you could listen to the latest sounds,
sitting on low chairs. In this room there was a bar, where
we served any type of drink you wanted. Next door in the
bedroom was the casino. The only furniture in the
bedroom was a table with chairs, where people sat and
played poker. Then, there was the kitchen at the end,
where the cooking went on. In the kitchen I employed a
man called Bully. He cooked Caribbean soul food, which
was rice and peas. In the front room would be some nice
jazz going down, with people drinking and smoking
dope. I would roll the joints out myself, and sell them for
five shillings a spliff. While the men were gambling, the
chicks sat around getting stoned and drunk. The gambling
room was mainly occupied by pimps where they would
gamble their night's wages away. There were also some
professional gamblers, who, more often than not, would
win the pimp's money from them. The game played was

five-card stud poker, with quite heavy stakes of up to £100 - a lot of money those days. The Shebeen had no fixed hours and just stayed open each day until the last people left. In any card game, the house is always a guaranteed winner, and on a good week, my Shebeen could earn up to £400. It was big money but it was a tightrope, because at any time you could get busted by the police for not having a licence. There were no fights, as such, down in Ladbroke Grove. There was no gangster protection, it was more 'peace and love', with the occasional screaming match, over a lost card game. My Shebeen became known as 'Johnny's Place'. My Landlord was the notorious slum property owner, Peter Rachman. Rachman, had made his money by buying properties with sitting tenants, and then viciously forcing them to leave.

At that time a well-known hustler in that area, was a man called Lucky Gordon. Lucky Gordon some years later was to play a major part in my life. Lucky Gordon was a loud mouth, who was always after the latest girl on the scene. He had a vicious streak in him. He was a bully.

Lucky was always popping in and out of my Shebeen and as time went by he became a real nuisance, hanging around the gambling room, peering over players' shoulders. He never had any real money to play himself and as a result he alienated the other gamblers. One night, after he had been a nuisance, I had to tell him to leave, and as he did so, he threw a milk bottle through the window. Ranting and raving in the street, he threatened to go and tell the police exactly what was going on in my Shebeen. I couldn't report him to the police, because I was running the whole thing illegally: selling dope etc. In

breaking the window and screaming at me that night,
Lucky had done the damage to my little enterprise.

Over the next month or so, lots of my customers started
staying away. Word came through the grapevine about
Lucky's threats, and my trade started thinning out. Lucky
was a nuisance, but I wasn't into violence as such, and
decided that the aggravation now outweighed the profits.
I closed down the Shebeen, and a new phase of my life
was about to begin.

CHAPTER 8
JAZZ MOBILE

After the Shebeen, I somehow drifted into the jazz mobile business. In those days, the union rate for a jazz musician was around £3 per gig, but in London, the pay was even lower, at £2 per gig. Club owners would expect the musicians to play for next to nothing. Jazz is a type of music about love and dedication, but once you become a jazz musician, you find freedom in your music because it's inexhaustible.

My first jazz mate was a guy called Dizzy Reece. If Dizzy had a gig in Manchester, he would get paid £5 plus his train fare. What we used to do, was use Dizzy's train fare for petrol, and that's how my jazz mobile business started. I wasn't actually making any money, but I was a jazzman myself, and was glad to go along for the ride. At first, when I drove Dizzy, I only had a small car, but when I started driving Tubby Hayes, I got an estate car. From being a part-time favour to a friend, it developed into a full-time business, which although not very profitable, I enjoyed. Being with friends, and listening to the music I loved, was real cool. There was plenty of smoke about, and I had a spliff going day and night. Full of hash, I merged with the car, and could just drive through the night - forever. After each show, with all the other guys asleep in the car, I just put my foot down on the pedal all the way back to London. Every musician of that era knew me, and still tells the wild stories about the whole, crazy scene. Amongst the weird and wonderful people I met was Phil Seaman. Phil was a registered junky on heroin. Man he was a great drummer - a very outspoken guy - but he loved his heroin. He was a greedy junky, who couldn't get enough junk in the intermission of each show. Looking for his drug fix, he would often miss the restart of each performance, so they had to quickly get a local drummer to fill in.

Sadly, Phil is dead. Tubby Hayes wrote and dedicated a number in honour of Phil Seaman called the `Late One`.

Tubby was tubby, white and Jewish, and played in his group with three others. Like so many of us, Tubby became a junk freak. Rumours go that some chick got him on the gear in the first place. Amongst the other guys I drove were: Count Basie, Fad Jones, Joe Williams and Dizzy Gillesby. I met many musicians through Dizzy like: Quincey Jones, Major Holy, Donald Byrd and Kenny Lynch. In those days, there weren't so many black guys hanging around together in the West End, so we stuck together in the Jazz Clubs.

Jazz and dope are the same, and at the time, were considered a real threat to society. So, for me to switch over from Jazz mobile to dope, was just a natural thing. Instead of listening to jazz, I now devoted my time to selling dope. My main customers were the black GI`s, the American service men, who came up to London from the army bases at the weekend.

They hung around with the other black Londoners, and they felt comfortable in clubs like, the 'All Nighter' or 'The Roaring 20`s'. GI`s had plenty of money, and were the best dope customers you could get.

And so was my life: dope dealing, dope smoking, dope talking, and dope sleeping, until the spring of 1962, when I was to meet a very foxy chick.

Her name was Christine Keeler.

Daily Mirror

WAR MINISTER SCANDAL

"I have come to realise that, by this deception, I have been guilty of a grave misdemeanour"

PROFUMO QUITS
He lied to MPs over Christine to save his family

Mirror Comment

THE BIG LIE

THE Daily Mirror does not kick a man when he is down.

Mr. Profumo, who married a beautiful and pleasant woman, is now down and out.

There can be nothing but pity for a man who has misled politician who has to admit—in a letter to his Prime Minister—that he is guilty of lying, of misleading of deception, and of a grave misdemeanour. The words of the confession were chosen by Profumo himself.

God knows, he was never a great Minister. It seems now that he is not a very important man. But there is guilt in many a human heart, and skeletons in many cupboards.

The question is:

What the hell is going on in this country?

Morals

All power corrupts—and the Tories have been in power for nearly twelve years. They are certainly enduring their full quota of fallen men—whited sepulchres and off-white coveralls.

In the Commons, Mr. Profumo made a personal statement in March.

BEFORE THE STORM

Smiling happily, before the storm broke . . . Mr. John Profumo pictured with his beautiful wife, former actress Valerie Hobson. Now he is a Minister no longer. And his political career is in ruins.

By VICTOR KNIGHT

WAR MINISTER JOHN PROFUMO caused a political sensation last night by resigning from the Government.

In a dramatic letter to the Prime Minister Mr Profumo admitted that he lied to the Commons about his association with red-haired model Christine Keeler "to protect my wife and family."

This admission finally clears away the cloud of rumour and suspicion which has hung over the political scene for more than three months.

The first public hint at a scandal building up around 48-year-old Mr. Profumo came during a Commons debate in the early hours of March 22.

Christine Keeler

Three Labour M.P.s referred to rumours surrounding 26-year-old Miss Keeler, who was then pending evidence in an Old Bailey shooting case.

A few hours later Mr. Profumo made a personal...

any possible improper connection with Miss Keeler, Any legal action against anyone spreading these rumours...

Continued on Back Page

CHAPTER 9
MEETING KEELER

I first met Christine Keeler in September 1962. Why I was chosen to be the one can only be put down to destiny. If you now study the events of the previous year you can clearly see that somebody somewhere was putting together the jigsaw that was to ruin the Conservative Party and force a General Election.

Wrong place, wrong time, that was my fate. Even I will never know the absolute truth as to whether Lucky Gordon was the original target to create a situation where Keeler would be forced in court and Profumo would get exposed. Did Lucky Gordon get out of hand in kidnapping Keeler? I guess so. Did the authorities then deem Lucky Gordon too much of a wild card? Perhaps the madness slotted together just the way it was meant to, like the big bang that created the universe.

At the time I met Keeler I never knew any of the people involved except of course Lucky Gordon. He had never been anything special just a petty hustler and a bully that hung around with all the other Jamaicans in Ladbroke Grove. It was the same Lucky who had given me all the hassle with my Shebeen years before. I was amazed to find she was even associating with him. I was not surprised however to find that Keeler was petrified of Lucky Gordon after she told me how he had kept her a prisoner for two days, naked in his flat. Still traumatised over it all Christine thought that he was out to kill her. From the first moment we met I found Christine extremely attractive and I suppose in those first couple of days I was full of myself offering to protect Christine from Lucky. Christine of course hearing all this felt secure with me. To her I became a black minder protecting her from a black monster called Lucky Gordon.

Our first night together was at Christine's new secret flat in Sheffield Terrace. I call it a secret flat because only a handful of people knew where it was. It had to be that way because Lucky Gordon was still looking to hurt Christine. It was a small private late night party. Four of us had been drinking and smoking pot, and at around two-o'clock, I said I was going to split. Christine turned to me, and said,

"Do you have to go?"

The inevitable happened, and we ended up in bed together, had sex, and crashed out.

The following morning I came-to at about twelve o'clock, and was getting dressed and ready to leave, when Christine asked me once more, to stay. I did stay, and was to be her lover, practically non-stop for the next eight weeks. The plot started to thicken a few days later when a man named Tony called round with a delivery. It wasn't groceries.

It was a gun, a German Luger automatic revolver. Keeler paid the man, and he left. At first I was quite shocked and asked Christine what the gun was for. She told me it was to protect herself against Lucky Gordon.

"You'd better give me that," I said taking the gun off Keeler.

"Guns," I thought, "What am I getting myself into?"

Christine's luxury flat was on the first floor in Sheffield Terrace a very fashionable part of London between Kensington High Street and Notting Hill Gate. During the next month Christine and I hardly went out at all and when we did go out it was always separately. Christine occasionally went on yet another secret rendezvous with one of her sugar daddies whereas when I went out is was mainly to buy more dope in Ladbroke Grove.

I don't know how much hash Christine smoked before she met me, but during the time we were together she smoked every day. The dope made her talk a lot, and it was in that first week that I was to hear the whole story - or at least her version of it.

Every night high as a kite Christine talked and talked telling me the sordid details of all the characters involved in the Profumo soap opera. Christine was already in at the deep end. I suppose she knew so much and had bottled it up for so long that me plus the dope was like a daily therapeutic session where she could confess everything. The stories varied from night to night but regardless of Christine's mood they basically all described the same mess. I don't think Christine remembered from one day to the next what she had told me because she often repeated herself.

The main player in her saga had to be Stephen Ward. Up to that time I had never met this man but listened intently

as Christine went on and on about him. Stephen Ward
was an osteopath who had munovered himself up
London's aristocratic social ladder. Stephen had
medically treated a host of famous people including
Prince Philip, Winston Churchill and numerous others.
Christine went on to tell me how Stephen made a habit of
befriending attractive young girls who worked in
nightclubs. Apparently she herself had met him shortly
after she had come to London while she was working in
'Murray's Cabaret Club'.

Stephen introduced these girls to influential men for sex.
One of these important men was John Profumo, the war
minister. At first I didn't know if Christine was talking
about other girls or herself as she went on to describe
somebody having sex with these high ranking people.

"Those toffs feel safe with us," she laughed. "We're
Wards girls."

Who she was actually referring to I didn't know but night
after night I just sat back smoked my joint and listened to
more. It was like watching a movie: the plot thickened
everyday. Christine went on to explain that government
ministers felt far safer having sex with one of Wards girls
as opposed to picking up a total stranger in a club or in
the street and putting their career and reputation at risk. I
was later to meet Stephen Ward and can categorically say
that he did not look to earn money directly out of these
girls. He wasn't your regular pimp. Stephen Ward in fact
was a pimp extraordinaire.

I was to find out later his fee was government secrets at
the highest level. For the right favour and useful

introductions he supplied sex. Stephen Ward's only problem was that he was now juggling so many balls in the air in such an intricate fashion that something had to drop. It eventually did on his head. Exactly what Stephen Ward was up to puzzles everybody even to this day. In those first few days listening to Christine I wondered whether all her stories were fact but as she went on I realised it was all-true.

Player number two was a Russian named Captain Yevgeny Ivanov. He had come to England as a naval attaché in 1960. I later discovered that he was deeply involved in the Keeler affair a long time before he ever went to bed with her. He was a secret service agent and was here to discover information about when England was to give Germany the bomb. Christine told me the whole story of the afternoon at 'Cliveden' the home of Lord Astor. It was while she was swimming naked in the pool on the country estate that Stephen had introduced her to Profumo and Ivanov. Stephen Ward orchestrated the meetings between Ivanov, John Profumo and of course Christine Keeler.

"Those Russians fucked well," Keeler laughed. "Perhaps its part of their training, in Moscow."

I laughed back saying, "I'll join the Russian secret service. I wouldn't mind training like that."

Christine had another joint and went on about other Russians but some of it became confusing and I didn't really follow what she was talking about.

Player number three was John Profumo.

"He's the war minister. He knows where the bombs are."

"Bombs!" I thought taking a draw on my smoke, "What the fuck's going on here?" Even then, though I was pretty stoned, there was a big part of me telling myself to get the fuck out before it was too late. The other part of me looked at this beautiful white chick that by now, even after just a few days, I was in love with.

Bombs or no bombs, I was staying!

Christine continued, "Jack knows everybody. He's had dinner with the Queen. He knows the Prime Minister personally. He once took me to his house." Christine boasted about Profumo, where they'd had sex and how the risk of it all was a turn on.

"I had never heard Profumo's name before but fuck if he knew where atomic bombs were and he'd had dinner with the Queen he must be quite important."

Player four was Lucky Gordon. At last we were talking about someone I knew.

"He tried to kill me. He's going to kill me and Stephen Ward." Christine became hysterical.

"He's going to kill us both. Lucky Gordon is looking for us everywhere now."

"He won't kill me," I replied. "That's for sure."

"I don't mean you I mean me and Stephen Ward. He's after us both" Christine went on and on. When I look back I realise how much Lucky Gordon himself was in love with Christine Keeler but Lucky was a real wild card and you couldn't control him. Lucky smoked a lot of dope and as a result of that his behaviour was always very erratic.

Although Lucky Gordon didn't frighten me it was the opposite with Christine and this Stephen Ward character. They were petrified of him. Exactly why they had ever become involved with Lucky I don't know but at that time they were both very frightened. I couldn't understand why Christine or this posh oeastiophath friend of hers wasn't going to the police to complain about Lucky Gordon. But a week later I was to meet Stephen Ward and find out exactly why.

Stephen Ward came to visit us one night in Sheffield Terrace. At first I thought that Stephen was Christine's lover but if he had been her lover that had long passed. They were now well involved with each other's lives but it wasn't sex, it was secrets Government secrets regarding the atomic bombs. Stephen Ward seemed extremely relieved that I was staying with Keeler. That evening he told me how they were both petrified of Lucky Gordon and Stephen now saw me as a protector. When I look back I realise now that Stephen Ward and myself like so many others were both deeply in love with Christine. Men didn't just sleep with Christine they fell in love with her. With Stephen it was not a sexual thing. He wanted to own Christine like a prize possession. Apparently he was once heard saying,

"When I found Christine she was a dancer at Murray's Cabaret Club. Look at who she sleeps with now."

The phone was always ringing. Christine and Stephen Ward both acted like they were in the middle of some world crisis. I wasn't completely sure what was going on but I could feel the tension. It was amazing the people they were talking about Harold Wilson: and the Prime Minister, Harold Macmillan. It was when I heard President Kennedy's name that I really started to listen. I started smiling and thought.

"Oh, fuck! President Kennedy and Lucky Gordon: there's a strange mix."

They were obviously in deep, deep, shit but I couldn't stop laughing, because in the middle of all the drama was this character I knew, Lucky Gordon a local hustler, trying to kill them.

I would laugh to myself at night. Atom bombs, Presidents of America, Prime Ministers and that Jamaican hustler, how did he become part of this crowd?

For them in the middle of their wars I suppose I really was the perfect answer: a black minder.

Stephen stayed until the early hours of the morning and, as he was leaving, talked privately with me giving me his phone number in case Lucky caused any new problems.

We didn't see Stephen Ward again for a few days but fuelled by the dope Christine's revelations continued. The main topic of conversation seemed to always focus on Profumo. In hindsight I think when Christine had first met Profumo, she believed it was by chance, but as time went on, she found out otherwise.

Even though she was a naive teenage girl, she began to realise that the whole thing had been very carefully orchestrated. By Stephen Ward in liaison with someone in the Labour Government?

Who will ever know the whole truth?

The sixties was a weird period. It really was the beginning of drugs. At least that's how it felt to me. I cannot say about all the politicians at that time, but everybody I knew, was on one drug or another. Sex in those days was totally liberated, the pill had come out, and we were all just fucking each other. Christine Keeler was not exactly looking for regular office work when she came to London, but in fairness to her, I think she was just sucked into the saga. Vulnerable people living on the edge are always at risk. Keeler was certainly living on the edge.

Come to think of it so was I!

Christine told me some stories about wild sex parties that were hard to believe! Famous names were involved, and you would think they were putting themselves at a great risk. Perhaps, in those top government circles, there was a secret sex club, a bit like a Masonic Lodge. If you were a member of this club, you could safely have sex with whom you wanted, and join in all the wild parties, without fear of being exposed.

Those clubs probably were such a closed shop, that no outsiders ever got in, to blackmail you.

There was, however, an unavoidable weakness.

Government circles are not exactly over crowded with eighteen-year-old girls, who were happy to sleep with ministers three times their age. Here was the big security flaw.

In any sex party, you had to have young girls. Young girls like Christine Keeler.

During the first few weeks at Sheffield Terrace apart from Stephen Ward no-one ever visited the flat. It was like we were in a world of our own on a cloud of hash. I would go out late at night and score enough dope to last for several days only to find it had run out by the following morning. We really were smoking one hell of a lot of dope. We must have gone out to buy food at some stage but I can't really remember where. I don't think we ate that much. We were too busy fucking and talking. It was around then that the mystery visitor started to come to the flat. At first he only came in the afternoon and while he was there I would go out.

By now I was totally obsessed with Christine Keeler and I would have done anything for her. Here I was with a gorgeous chick and in the beginning it was like a fairy tale dream. Little did I know then that dream was to become a living nightmare. Sexually, she was very good, but to add to the turn-on, she had loads of money.

Also, the mystery of me being sent out of the flat, for two or three hours at a time, while she entertained this important man, was in itself, like some big game.

One day the bell rang and it was one of Christine's sugar daddies.

"Oh God I forgot he was coming. Quick, you've got to hide." Christine said panicking.

I did and got into the cupboard. I had to listen to all the heavy breathing and sighs of pleasure. I was jealous but there was nothing I could do other than stay in the cupboard.

After they had sex I heard the man talking. He was worried about something he had said to her and was quizzing her to find out if she had spoken to anyone. They left the room and I couldn't hear the rest of the conversation.

After he had gone we smoked a joint and Christine told me that the man who I had just listened to was the War Minister Profumo.

That night we had sex. I smiled to myself thinking, "I wonder whose better in bed, me, Profumo or Kennedy?"

The following evening I decided to go to 'The All Nighters Club.' I used to spend most weekends there and everyone knew me. The 'All Nighters Club' was an enormous basement club, in Wardour Street, opposite Gerard Street. At the weekends the club was packed with about two hundred people listening to the top jazz musicians. There was no alcohol licence in the club but if you were in the know you could buy a coca cola and you'd get a whisky in it. You had to be in the 'in crowd', however, to get those special drinks. As much as I was in love and infatuated with Keeler I was quite happy to get out and about again and be back amongst the clubbers. Coming back one night from the club I got out of a cab in

Sheffield Terrace and found Stephen Ward waiting for me in his car.

"I have got to talk to you. I'm desperate. Come with me. I must talk to you now."

We got in the car and Stephen drove round the corner. I remember it so clearly we parked somewhere by Pembroke Square. Stephen Ward had his back against the wall. He looked worried like he was in deep shit.

"I'm going to prison for life I'm going to be arrested for espionage. You have got to help me because Christine will go to prison as well."

He kept repeating himself over and over again. He told me the whole story. He was like a man in a sinking ship. He was desperate. A lot of what he said didn't make absolute sense but he was in a bad way. Although I didn't know Stephen Ward very well for some reason I wanted to help. I was in love with Christine who was my main concern and didn't want anything to happen to her but I really liked Stephen Ward. There was something about him that appealed to me.

That night in his car I didn't understand what it was all about. It was only later that the pieces of the jigsaw started fitting together and this is how they fitted.

The Profumo/Keeler saga didn't all begin on day one and finish on day twenty. The saga started and as the sordid messy details evolved opportunists from all walks of life stepped in to attack or defend the situation. And that is exactly how it was. The Labour government knew what was going on and were now strongly on the attack. Several political chess players who had originally sided with one party were now changing sides. Stephen was very nervous, a bit like he'd done something and been caught red handed. It was as if, in an irrational manner, he was trying to rectify everything in one foul swoop. Only he and I will ever know the details of our conversation but when I look back I realise he was in deep, deep shit.

I was there at the time and with everything I saw and heard this is my take on the story, which believe me will be pretty accurate.

It was Stephen Ward who orchestrated Keeler in bed with Profumo to ask for the nuclear weapons secrets. Stephen was obviously selling these secrets. Either that or his political alliance was firmly to Russia. Stephen passed the information to Ivanov. This was high treason. A charge of treason is as serious as murder and a traitor can go to prison for forty years. Someone high up in the Labour government had found out and had informed Harold Wilson as to what had gone on. Harold Wilson or his gang now had four wonderful moves on the Profumo/Keeler chessboard.

Move one: confront Stephen Ward and tell him there is enough evidence to put him in prison for forty years. This meant Christine Keeler would also have gone to prison for a long time. Whilst making these early moves relax quietly on the backbenches, in opposition, knowing your checkmate is only three more moves away.

Move two: do a deal with Stephen Ward, to get Keeler into court, as a witness, where she can be cross-examined.

Move three: in cross-examination insure that leading Conservative ministers are exposed and disgraced sufficiently to get the public's vote of no confidence.

Move four: check mate! Early election and new job as Prime Minister.

Some politicians are like drug addicts they are addicted not to drugs but to power and do not want to spend their career sitting on the backbenches. They will do anything and everything to get into power.

In the car that night Stephen, practically in tears, told me somebody high up in the labour government, had been to see him with a senior police officer, with concrete evidence that Keeler on his instructions had got military secrets from Profumo which had been passed on to the Russians. Stephen couldn't stop talking. He was paranoid and at his wits end was now suspecting everybody. He was talking like a deranged man in a very desperate situation.

Stephen was clearly so upset and worried I don't think he fully realised what he was saying or whom he was saying it to.

"Oh, Fuck this was all so far above my head I was just a happy, dope smoking, hustler from the Caribbean Islands and now I was being linked with high treason and espionage.

"Will you help me and Christine?" he pleaded.

"If Christine goes to prison she'll be an old woman before she gets released," he said now practically in tears.

Because I was in love with Christine I agreed to help and we arranged to meet the following evening in the Queens way.

"You must never mention our meeting to Christine. She will only worry too much and do something else stupid," he said sternly.

He went on to promise

"If you do as I tell you, you and Christine can live in luxury. Neither of you will ever have to work again."

As I write this book today I wonder why I didn't just walk away. I didn't and I was to pay the price.

Something strange was going on but I didn't really fully understand what it was or the severity of it all. When I went back that night to Sheffield Terrace Christine Keeler seemed different, very tense and wouldn't come off the phone. Deep down I knew that now everything was out of control.

I had led an eventful life so far, and believed that this whole Keeler affair was just another crazy episode - on a cloud of hash.

I just thought it would all end, without any major drama, and blend in with the next period of my life.

How wrong I was to be.

CHAPTER 10
STEPHEN WARD

Later that evening I was once again smoking dope with Keeler back at Sheffield Terrace. In between phone calls Christine rambled on to me in her usual way. But it was different now because I had become directly involved. I was now my own independent player on the Profumo/Keeler chessboard.

I now had my own secret moves that even Christine didn't know about. I can't say for certain why I did what I did but I was in love with Keeler and certainly didn't want her to go to prison for forty years. I suppose it's true to say I wasn't just in love with Keeler but with the lifestyle that seemed to be on offer with her. Anyway as history shows I went along with it all.

The following night I met Stephen as arranged. He was waiting for me in his car parked behind Whitley's store in the Queensway.

As I got in he pushed a gun in my hand!

"Fuck man what are we going to do, kill some body?" I asked.

"No, no, no nobody is going to get killed. It's all very simple. All you have to do is take this gun on Friday night, when you are alone with Keeler, fire the gun all over the flat at the ceiling and leave the rest to me."
I was shocked!

"Oh no, I'm not firing no guns," I said.

"The very worst you'll get is a fine or three months in prison and in return for that Christine is yours for life." Stephen continued.

Stephen talked as if Christine was a possession that he could use as a pawn in any way he wanted. It was as if Stephen had the ultimate control and Keeler had to do what he said.

Stephen went on and on telling me how someone from the Labour Government was blackmailing him over a charge of espionage against him and Keeler.

"We will both go to prison for forty years!" he cried out.

Once again like the previous evening he became hysterical. He was sweating again as he pushed the gun at me again.

"No, no, I said I'll do it but I don't need your gun. I've got the gun Christine bought. I'll use that.

I wasn't going to fire any guns but I just wanted to get out the car and be on my own. It was only when I got outside and walked away that I began to realise the seriousness of what was actually going on. I went back to Sheffield Terrace, hardly slept all night and by morning even Christine could see there was something wrong with me.

I went out and spent the morning alone in Hyde Park. It is funny forty years later I can see myself so clearly sitting on a bench by the Serpentine Lake. I was smoking a joint telling myself to get the fuck out and split with this Keeler chick. If I had have done and Christine had gone to prison for espionage as Stephen Ward was predicting, then with no remission she would be being released this year in September 2002.

For me it was a fast moving time and when asked why I stayed I would say it was because of my love for Christine Keeler. That morning in the park I decided to stay with Keeler but there is no way I was going to fire any guns.

Friday night came and around 8 o'clock the phone rang. Keeler was out so I answered it. It was Stephen Ward.

"What's going on?" said Stephen down the phone.

"I've been thinking about it and I don't want to get involved," I replied.

I was very apprehensive about the whole thing now, and after telling Stephen Ward a second time that I definitely didn't want any part of it, I put the phone down.

About ten minutes later Keeler came back and seeing her I said,

"We are going out to the All Nighters Club."

Earlier that day I had arranged to meet two of my buddies there and thought it was safe to take Christine as Lucky was barred from the club. Christine didn't know what had gone on between Stephen Ward and myself and I never mentioned the telephone call to her. With the idea of going to the club Christine seemed relieved and anxious at the same time.

"What if Lucky Gordon's about and he attacks me?"

"He won't bother you at all. I'll be with you the whole time and besides he's barred from the club," I assured her.

"Shall we bring the gun with us?" Christine asked.

"Guns! Fucking guns! I don't care what we do. I just want to get out and listen to some jazz man."

We caught a cab and twenty minutes later we were in the 'All Nighters Club'. With the music going full blast we drank a few whiskeys and smoked some joints. It seemed for the time being our troubles were all over.

And that's how life carried on and over the next few days it all went quiet. We smoked our dope and most nights met up in the club after Keeler finished doing what ever she was doing.

CHAPTER 11
THE KRAY TWINS

The next few weeks of my life were very confusing, very fast moving, and as I reflect back they mingle into one another.

It's funny, but that whole period of the sixties was like some sordid jigsaw coming together, with dead bodies about to be found on both sides of the Atlantic. I never actually saw Christine Keeler sleep with President Kennedy, but I sure heard a lot of rumours. In August of 62, Marylyn Monroe was found dead, and her death left many unanswered questions regarding the Kennedy brother's sexual activities. In London meanwhile, the main gossip was more about the man in the mask. At all the high class sexually perverted gatherings there was a very well known man who would prance about naked wearing a mask. Even if I knew categorically who the man in the mask was, I doubt whether I would have the courage to expose him. Pat Marlow, a top call girl, who did know the identity of the man in the mask, was found dead in her London flat.

Early in October 1962, reports were begining to come in to the security services, that Stephen Ward was supplying girls for sex, to top government officials. One of these girls was my lover and bed mate - Christine Keeler.

Christine started going out a lot more at night now. And we began meeting each other every day in the early hours of the morning in the 'All Nighters Club'

One night, two white guys grabbed me outside as I was arriving at the club, and marched me around the corner to put me in the back of a car.

One of the men was Scottish and he spoke first. He said he was with the Kray twins and I should take notice of what they were saying. The Krays themselves were not there but these two guys looked real evil.

"I understand you're living with this girl."

He pulled out a photograph of Christine Keeler, who was pictured coming out of some building. I was a bit stoned at the time, and my reply was something like,

"What's up man? I can live with a chick, can't I?"

I had never had direct dealings with the Krays before, but this was heavy shit, and I did not feel too easy about it. It was a serious situation.

"We've got a job for you, Johnny Boy. We know where you live. And we know a lot of people who know you. And I am sure on that basis we can work together quite well."

The other man, a shorter red headed chap, asked me about Christine's movements.

Then leaning towards the back of the car staring at me he said,

"Stephen Ward told you what to do. Now just fucking do it if you want to stay alive!"

I got out of the car and went back into the 'All Nighters Club' in Wardour Street. I was in so much shock that I just flopped down. I needed a strong spliff but luckily I already had one rolled.

I realised then that I was already involved in something very deep, and it was too late to get out of it.

An hour or so later, Keeler came into the club, and her first words were,

"Hi Johnny baby, d'you have a smoke for me?"

That night the two of us got really stoned, went to bed and had sex.

The next morning when we woke up, remembering everything from the day before, I was shocked and I thought to myself, "No, no I don't want to get myself involved anymore in all of this but what the fuck can I do?"

I didn't tell Keeler anything but wanting to keep out of more trouble for the next few days we stayed in the flat. Sometime towards the end of October Christine told me she was going to the hairdressers. I asked her where the hairdressers were she told me it was in the Grove.

"You shouldn't go down there you could run into Lucky." I warned her.

She wouldn't listen and left to get her hair cut in Comeragh Road. While she was out of all the people in the world to bump into she came face to face with Lucky

Gordon in the street. He went berserk and started punching her. I don't know exactly how but some strangers interrupted and she managed to escape into a taxi and came back very shaken to Sheffield Terrace.

Over the next week the rumours coming in through the grapevine about Lucky's new threats were getting worse, so Christine and I moved in to a new flat, in Lancaster Gate. The location of this flat was kept a strict secret and our only visitors were my close friends, Ralph and Anne, who coincidently lived in the flat below. Now, Keeler just stayed at home with me most of the time getting stoned. When she did go out it was a cab door to door.

The beginning of the end was foreseeable on October 27th. Ironically the same day as the Cuban Missile Crisis reached its climax, Lucky Gordon was badly cut. At that time, these two incidents seemed completely unconnected, but for some politicians, the aftermath was to become very definitely connected.

It all happened one night in the 'All Nighters Club'. Tubby Hayes was playing, and I was standing up, diggin' the music with Christine and a few other people. At that moment Lucky came in, looking very intimidating. There were about four people in our party, and I was standing up by a rail, which separated the seating area from the dance floor. I was listening to the music when Lucky came up and punched me. I jumped over the table to go after him, but Lucky grabbed a chair. Then the bouncer grabbed Lucky and dragged him out of the club and into the foyer. There was a scuffle, during which Lucky got cut. Shortly after, Christine and I left the club in a hurry. We went to a nearby Shebeen in Powis Terrace, in

Ladbroke Grove. At the Shebeen, the owner told us that Lucky had just been there with the police, looking for us.

Like Bonnie and Clyde, Christine and I were now on the run and arranged to stay with a friend of mine, called Manfred, who lived in Brentford. It was all closing-in on me, and closing-in fast, and there was nothing I could do about it. Now the police were involved.

Lucky needed fourteen stitches in his face and later when they were removed he put them in a box and posted them to Keeler at Wimpole Mews saying that for each one she would get two in her face.

CHAPTER 12
I SHOT THE SHERIFF

First we went to collect a few clothes from Lancaster Gate. We then took a cab to Brentford, where for the first few days, like two fugitives, we did not go out at all. But by the following week, with no police or Lucky Gordon banging at the door, we began to feel safer. By now, I was deeply in love with Christine and would like to believe that she was in love with me.

While the political scandal gathered momentum in Westminster and the Russian spy Ivanov was passing his secrets in Knightsbridge, Christine and I just got stoned in Brentford. For several days we just got stoned, had sex, got stoned again, had sex again – only occasionally stopping for a break, a cup of tea or something to eat. Neither of us knew what time it was, or even what day it actually was. It was irrelevant.

All good things must come to an end though, and my final love interlude with the seductive Christine Keeler suddenly finished, due to outside pressure. Christine had been on the phone to Michael Eddows a solicitor she'd met through Stephen Ward, and whatever he was saying to her, seemed to be causing a great deal of panic. Even before that telephone call, I had noticed Christine was getting itchy feet and started talking about going back to central London. Michael Eddows was offering Christine a flat, on her own, in Regents Park. The deal was that I didn't live with her. I didn't want Christine to leave but she insisted. Her idea was she should go to the new flat for a day or so. This way she could find me a solicitor for advice, regarding the warrant, now out for me, over the Lucky Gordon fight. Meanwhile in Brentford I was to lay low and keep out of sight until Christine got help.

"You stay here. I will still see you each week," she continued.

Christine wanted to have her cake and eat it. She wanted me to still see her once or twice a week, but I was upset that she was leaving me. I felt my use was over and she was deserting me for someone. I became very upset and shouted,

"If you just want a black stud, go down the Grove! There are plenty of black men that will fuck you when you want!"

Christine was taking all her clothes out of the wardrobe, when she dropped my tie on the floor. She refused to pick it up. Tempers were boiling over and I got very angry. Now we were both shouting and I threatened to smack her, unless she picked up my tie. In spite of the fact that Christine had a lot of money like most men I wanted to be the boss and stupidly believed that Christine was doing what I said. I told her again,

"Pick my tie up now!"

Her reply was,

"You don't get angry when I fuck other men, but you get angry when I won't pick up your tie!"

A row followed, and Christine stormed out of the house and got a cab back to town.

I was very angry, and felt betrayed that Christine was dumping me for her solicitor. I was furious. I should have killed the bitch. With hindsight, if I had have killed Keeler, the whole scandal would not have come out. The Conservatives would have stayed in power, and Harold Wilson would have been well fucked. He would never have smoked that stupid pipe outside Downing Street in the first place.

Here I was now, in an impossible no win situation. Christine had gone. I was alone in Brentford. So I did the usual and lit a joint, and reflected on what was.

The Krays henchmen were looking for me.

Lucky Gordon was looking for me.

The police were looking for me.

Fuck knows who else was looking for me that I didn't know about.

On top of all this, my chick had deserted me for her posh solicitor.

Christine was now smoking dope heavily and in those days, dope dealers were not so easy to find. She couldn't go down the Grove to score anymore, still feeling petrified of Lucky Gordon attacking her again. Instead the bitch actually had the cheek to ring Manfred, the guy I was staying with in Brentford, to score her some more dope! The following day when Manfred told me he was taking dope to Christine, I just shrugged my shoulders. That night, when Manfred drove into town with Christine's dope, I asked him to take me into town as well. I was still hurting and didn't want to see Christine. I wanted to visit Anne and Ralph's at their flat in Lancaster Gate. Even though there was still a warrant out for me, for cutting Lucky Gordon, at the Lancaster Gate flat, I felt safe. Anne and Ralph were trusted old friends. Manfred dropped me outside and I went into Anne and Ralph's alone. The three of us smoked dope and swallowed some 'blues' amphetamine tablets. We had been up all night, when at around 7am, with the three of us high as a kite, the telephone rang.

It was Christine Keeler.

She went absolutely mad, screaming at Anne,

"You're fucking my old man you slag! You tell that bastard John Edgecombe I am going to punish him. I am not going to get him a solicitor and what's more I am going to tell the police it was him who cut Lucky Gordon's face!"

Christine was genuinely jealous and I thought that this confirmed we were in love. I assumed Christine's jealousy was because she wanted me back with her and she was at Brentford looking for me. I got a cab back to the house in Brentford only to find it empty. By now I was really up tight and frantically started to phone everywhere, trying to track down Christine. It was early in the morning and I had been up all night on blues. Eventually, I got through to Stephen Ward's flat in

Wimpole Mews and Mandy Rice-Davies answered the telephone. Mandy said that Christine was not there, but I sensed that she was. I started screaming,

"Don't give me all that bullshit, I know she's there!"

By now I was fuming. Christine's gun was hidden under my trousers, which were hanging in the wardrobe. Like a desperado, I just grabbed the pistol not even considering the actual consequences of carrying a loaded gun. I wasn't thinking straight. I was too fucking mad over this Christine bitch withdrawing her help, and now threatening to shop me to the police. This was what the Krays and Stephen Ward had wanted, and now in my insanity, I was actually giving it to them. I called a cab and we drove to Wimpole Mews. I didn't speak to the driver on the drive into town. I just sat there the whole way brooding.

At Wimpole Mews I rang the bell. Mandy came to the window, and I screamed,

"Tell Christine I'm here. I know she's up there!"

At first, Mandy denied that she was there, but I kept on and on, and eventually Christine came to the window. I shouted,

"Come on downstairs and talk to me!"

She refused and said, "No we will talk from here."

I started screaming, "You're wasting my time. This cab is costing me money."

At this, Christine threw a pound note out the window.

This was the point that my world exploded.

I just went mad and blew my cool. I began shouldering the front door, but it was a real tough door, and after the first time, I knew the door was not going to budge. Like a gangster, I thought, "OK, I'll shoot the door off." So I wiped out my shooter and started firing at the lock.

Bang! Bang! Bang! Bang! Bang!

I fired five shots at the door, but it wouldn't budge. Christine was now back at the window, and began pleading with me,

"Johnny don't be silly! The police are going to come and you'll get into trouble."

These were the last words my lover, Christine, ever said to me, in my entire life. I would so much like to believe that those words, "Johnny you'll get into trouble", were meant genuinely regarding my safety, and that whatever we had going on between us, in that short space of time, was real.

I would like to believe that, in our crazy mixed up world, all those years ago, in the middle of the Profumo scandal, Christine and I had found true love.

I was still trying to break down the door and Christine came back to the window.

"You bitch! This is all your fault!" I shouted out.

I looked up, and oblivious to the gun in my hand, I pointed at her. At this point, the gun went off. Christine, now convinced, I was going to murder her, vanished inside the flat. Now I was in real trouble, and without thinking, hid the gun in the back garden. I then jumped back in the cab, and off we drove.

How much of it was drugs, how much of it was fear and obeying the Kray's and Stephen Wards orders I don't know. But one thing is for sure, in firing those shots, the Krays had been obeyed, and the Labour Party had got what they wanted. Harold Wilson's Government would soon be in power.

"Take me back to Brentford and quick! Don't stop," I shouted at the driver. On the way back his car radio sounded. It was his office, wanting to talk to him. The police were already in the mini-cab office and one of them spoke to the driver, to ask him whom he had in his cab.

It was like a scene from a movie, as this voice came out over the cab radio,

"Have you got a man called John Edgecombe in your cab?"

"Yes," the driver replied.

"Don't try to apprehend him because he is a very dangerous man."

I interrupted, "Switch off that radio and just keep driving."

"No problem," came back the reply from the driver, who had now switched off the radio, and was now racing along like a lunatic.

I wanted to get back to the Brentford house as quickly as possible, to get rid of the spare bullets, which were hidden there. I had hoped by doing this, there would be no evidence against me. On arriving at Brentford, I dashed into the house and put the bullets in my pocket. I was ready to escape, but before I could get back out in the street, the police were at the door. Suddenly Manfred's mother was now in the hall. She thought I had another gun and shouted out,

"Johnny don't do anything silly!"

For several minutes the police just stood there, facing me in the passage. They must have been thinking that I was about to pull out a gun and shoot them.

We all froze - just staring at each other. Then the police officers grabbed me in a neck lock. They were all shouting at me to tell them where the gun was.

While we were all struggling, a message came through on their radio that a gun had been found behind Stephen's flat. I was now handcuffed, and taken to the local police station. The minicab driver was also taken with us. I told the police he wasn't involved in any way, and that he was just a mini cab driver. Sometime later they let him go.

The police began to interrogate me and wanted to know exactly what had happened. Nobody would ever really know, not even me. That day I was very stoned, and high on blues and dope, obviously I didn't know exactly what I was doing. I knew what I had been told to do, over the years many people have asked me why I shot those bullets.

I will let you be the judge of that, because whatever I say, it will still leave a big question mark.
You choose. The three versions are

I was so stoned that I didn't know what I was doing.
I was very upset that my lover had left me. I had taken too many drugs, and high as kite, I just shot the gun, like a spoilt little child trying to get attention.

I was so angry that I wanted to kill her.
My lover had left me to sail of into the sunset with some white government minister, and on the basis that I could not have her, no one else could, and I intended to shoot her dead.

I was obeying Ronnie Kray's and Stephen Ward's orders to get them off my back.
Petrified of the Krays, I was obeying them. This way, at least the Krays would have been off my back, and Harold Wilson would have been off the Kray's back.

If I had actually shot Christine dead and the scandal had never come out, would Prufumo have become Prime Minister? Would there have been an extra appreciative pay-off from the Conservative Government, to Ronnie Kray? Would Ronnie himself have given up crime, and possibly gone into politics - maybe become Home Secretary? Who knows, but with the state of England today, and its broken down railways, hospitals and schools, perhaps Ronnie Kray might have done a better job.

Anyway the shots were fired and the scandal door was now wide wide open.

CHAPTER 13
BRIXTON PRISON

I was arrested on the 14th of December in Brentwood, and handcuffed in between two enormous policemen, taken to the local police station. Locked in a cell, I could hear the excitement as the local policemen realized guns were involved and that this was an attempted murder charge. It was the most exciting thing they had ever dealt with. An hour later, I was driven to Marylebone Police Station in London, where after being charged, I was held for the night. My mind was in a haze and to this very day I cannot remember exactly what I was initially charged with.

The following morning I was taken to Marlborough Street Magistrates Court, where the charges were read out and I was remanded in Brixton Prison.

"Shit," I thought.

Had I been charged with murder, treason, kidnapping, or drug dealing? One thing was for sure, it certainly wasn't shoplifting."

In Brixton prison they always kept the murderers totally separate from other convicts, and because I was on some kind of murder charge, I was automatically put in the locked 'Psycho Unit', along with all the other killers.

Unlike a normal cell, where three prisoners would share a small space, the Psycho Unit was an enormous locked room, with rows of beds down either side. You slept at night with twenty other killers around you, constantly snoring and grunting. Many of them murmured in their sleep, shouting things like, "Die you bastard, die!"

During those first few nights, expecting to be stabbed to death in my sleep, I hardly closed my eyes.

The Psycho Unit was like a murderer's social club and often prisoners sat around big tables having tea and discussing the actual ways that they had committed their murders. A lot of the men had committed crimes of passion killing their wives or girlfriends, and had been caught red-handed. So, in most cases there was no way they could say they were not guilty, which allowed them to talk about their killings quite openly, like it was gardening.

The conversations during afternoon tea often went something like this:

"Did you stab yours?"

"No. I battered her over the head."

"How many times did you have to hit her?"

"Oh, loads. They don't fucking die quickly."

"'Arry you battered yours as well didn't you?"

"Yep, that's how I did her," Harry replied, as he looked up from his newspaper.

"What d'you use? An 'ammer?"

"No, my son's Cricket bat. Fuckin' bat broke an' all didn't it. Expensive bat as well, cost me over £10."

And so the conversations went on and on.

The guy in the bed next to me was Harvey Smith, who, because of his jealousy, shot his wife six times. The man on the other side had killed a man over a football match result. I would just lie in bed, all day in that Psycho Unit, trying to work out exactly what I had done. During those early days, I certainly didn't need drugs to be in a stoned dream state - I was in it naturally.

I was kept in prison over Christmas, and on the 17th January I was taken back to Marlborough Street Magistrates Court, where I was charged with attempted murder and remanded in custody for trial at the Old Bailey. At the Marlborough Street Court, evidence was given against me and Christine Keeler was called to the witness box.

Handcuffed I looked over at Keeler. It felt very confusing seeing her all over again. She looked stunning and I still loved her. She wouldn't look over at me and that hurt me a great deal. Inside I was boiling over. Here was the girl I had spent so many passionate nights with now giving evidence against me. Was she doing all this because of the fear of an espionage charge?

With this and many more questions racing round my head the case started and Christine gave her evidence.

"He pointed the gun at me. I saw the bullet coming and I ducked."

Everybody started laughing, and while the laughter rang out around the whole court, I heard the words,

"Attempted murder!"

"Attempted murder!"

"Trial at the Old Bailey."

I was now in at the deep end. The Old Bailey only deals with the most serious cases.

I looked out again across the crowded courtroom towards Keeler. Christine caught my eye, but she turned away. I was numb.

Would I ever see her again?

I never did and to this very day that was the last I ever saw of Christine Keeler!

That morning in court, the 'Black Power Movement', who had somehow heard about my case, sent me an Indian Solicitor. This man and I looked like a circus standing there together. This Indian man stood up and actually asked to get me bail. The police and the magistrates once again laughed, signifying that it was a bloody cheek to even suggest it.

Stephen Ward, espionage Keeler getting 40 years - fuck what was going on?

It was rather late but I think it was now I began to want to protect myself but who would believe me.

I was so shocked with it all I think a part of me thought I could get charged myself with treason.

I couldn't think straight but even in my confused state, I realized that with me, a black man, alongside this Indian lawyer, we stood out too much amongst all the white barristers. I would stand a much better chance with a white English lawyer. With this in mind, I got rid of the Indian man and somehow was given a new white solicitor Irvin Shaw. At first I felt much safer with Irvin Shaw, but with hindsight, I now know that Irvin Shaw was yet another mistake. The way he was to act for me was as if he'd done a deal with the authorities. Too many famous names were involved in all this; too many heads were going to have to roll. When Profumo a short while later denied he had had sex with Keeler, Stephen Ward once again backed him up.

When Labour threatened espionage Ward had originally changed sides but even after he did Ward continued with a foot in both camps pretending he was siding with Profumo to keep Keeler silent.

Like a drowning man he was desperately trying to appease both sides paranoid of being charged by either party with espionage.

The Labour Government had thrown the dice with me firing that gun, and now the Conservatives were desperately defending their weakening position. It was a big political chess game.

At that stage the Conservatives believed they still had Stephen Ward playing ball and therefore the situation could be saved. I could be put away in prison perhaps without Keeler even having to appear in court. The whole thing could then have been closed, and they could all have gone home for tea. What the Conservative Government needed was a solicitor that would play ball with the prosecution. They needed to get me convicted, and somehow keep Keeler out of the witness box. They knew if Keeler was cross-examined, the whole scandal would come out. The Conservatives job now was to make sure that I went to prison without Keeler's evidence and stayed for a long time.

That initial court hearing was soon over and I was back sitting with my murderer friends in the Psycho Ward.

All the other prisoners gathered around me, eager to find out what had happened.

"Case referred to the Old Bailey," I blurted out.

"Fuck man! That's gonna be a long sentence. You're going' down for a long, long time," a frowning prisoner said.

Another prisoner commented, "You're gonna need a good brief, mate."

My new solicitor, Irvin Shaw, was now officially representing me, and he began to visit me in prison regularly. We always spoke in private, without a prison officer, and it wasn't long before I realized that the visits were not forming any part of my defence. Irvin Shaw was in fact interrogating me, to find out exactly what secrets I knew about Keeler's sex life.

During the eight weeks I was in Brixton Prison, I was in a bewildered state, not really knowing what was going on. I found out later that a lot of the same information I gave that bloody solicitor, Irvin Shaw, appeared in an Italian newspaper.

Every night lying in bed, listening to the murderers, I wondered what the fuck was a black dope-smoking guy like me, doing in this mess? Bits of news filtered in by word of mouth or newspapers, but while I was sweating it out in prison, outside two completely different webs were being woven.

The Krays didn't tell their men to order me to shoot a gun on a whim. They were obviously under instructions and getting payment from, somebody quite high up in government.

It was Keeler that had told the police exactly where to find me after the shooting, which I suppose, is understandable. It's not every day that somebody fires a gun at you. Whether Keeler thought I was actually trying to kill her, or just waving a gun, no one would ever really know, not even her. Only I know the truth. But she was frightened, and wanted to get me arrested as quickly as possible. The Krays and the Labour Party had got what they wanted. Me being arrested was the key that opened the scandal door.

I now had to appear in court and Keeler was the key witness to me shooting her. Obviously she would have to appear in court as well. In court, once she had given evidence against me, she would be cross-examined under oath. Now absolutely any question could be asked like,

"Do you think Edgecombe shot at you because he was jealous that you slept with Profumo?"

Under oath, Keeler would have to answer any question, about anybody. This was a catastrophe for the Conservative Party. All the bribes, all the threats, could not stop a criminal case coming to court once there was a charge of attempted murder. The Krays had done their job. A charge like this could only be stopped if there was insignificant evidence. The police had the evidence, Christine Keeler's statement. These statements were on police files and without a 'Watergate' type break-in, there was no way these records were going to go missing. Corruption comes at all levels but there is a limit. Even a Prime Minister cannot fix police files to go missing. Cases due to be heard in court cannot just vanish. In fact, it was easier to get rid of Keeler herself than the statements she had given. As soon as Keeler had said the very first words to the police, many top politicians were in deep shit. Not only were politicians in trouble, other people were about to die. Bar mass-murder, there was no longer anyway that this scandal was going to be swept under the carpet by anybody now.

It was a very funny situation, with possibly a hundred people being involved in the whole saga. Those people included: The Prime Minister Harold Macmillan, Christine Keeler, various call-girls, The Russian spy Ivanov, The Krays, Harold Wilson leader of the opposition, the President of the United States, two or three dope dealers, Stephen Ward and a host of others. A top fiction writer couldn't have dreamt up a better story.

As the days rolled on the Secret Services, were inundated on a daily basis with fresh rumours, some of which were substantial, some exaggerated, but they were all good rumours, and therefore they had to be listened to. The one fact that was immediately verified was that I had shot at Keeler. Now these investigators, in high-up places, wanted to know who had paid me, or who had forced me to shoot that gun. One rumour set off another, and like all types of gossip the whole thing got exaggerated. The truth itself was bad enough, but some of the stories coming in were even more far out.

One story was that Vassal, the spy, had slept with Ronnie Kray

The scandal had spread everywhere. In America there were rumours in the White House directly linking President Kennedy and Christine Keeler.

I hadn't exactly done what I was told to do, but in my madness I had acted out my orders at least. The end result was what the Labour government had wanted, the job was done and the scandal was now all out in the open.

Watergate and President Nixon seemed preposterous but that bag of worms came out too, and as a result, Nixon bit the dust. This was England's sex Watergate.

Sex is worse than any drug addiction. Those government ministers had an addiction to Sex. This can be simply explained as: when they saw a woman that they fancied,

regardless of the dangers, they had to have sex with her.
That woman's body becomes a drug, and having tasted it,
they had to go back for more and more.

If you were in politics and you had a competitor who had
done a bad job with the economy, you would use the
spiralling cost of living as bad publicity to disgrace the
opposition, get them out of power, and get yourself into
government. Equally if the opposition had been caught
having sex with somebody they shouldn't have, you
would rub your hands gleefully. Now you had the
ammunition to expose them, disgrace them, and put them
out of work. Crafty politicians however, would not wait
for the opposition to meet somebody; they would
orchestrate the sexual pleasure to be flaunted in front of
the minister. They could serve him up his choice of dish.
Homosexual, heterosexual, or group sex, even sadist type
sex-orgies, it was all on offer.

Trap him, get him disgraced and get him sacked, then at
the next election get his job.

That's exactly what happened in 1962.

To have War Ministers who liked young eighteen-year-
old dark haired girls was a liability to the Conservative
government. Rumour had it that the Conservative
government, however, also had lots more liabilities, with
many other ministers who favoured young boys. Stephen
Ward supplied the girls perhaps Ronnie Kray supplied
the boys, Max supplied the drugs and Mr… paid the bill.
Who knows what the fuck was really going on? That
being the case for Mr… the bill was not anywhere near as
expensive as a normal electioneering bill. I laugh now,

because I very much doubt whether Reggie or Ronnie Kray had any political allegiance, and more than likely at some time enforced favours for both governments at the same time. You can almost imagine Ronnie saying to Reggie during their morning meetings at Valance Road. "I don't like that cunt's policy on education."

The Labour party knew that Keeler being present in court, giving evidence against me, would have led to her being cross-examined, and then the whole story would have hit the news in a big way. This was their guarantee to bring down the Conservative government.

On February 1st 1963 the Conservatives were forced to make one of their last desperate moves. I was back in court, but my trial was somehow adjourned. The excuse given at the time was that the mini-cab driver who drove me to the shooting was sick, and therefore couldn't give evidence. I found out later though that he wasn't sick, he was scared for his life. The Conservatives used this to buy time, in order to get Keeler out of the country and on the missing list for good.

The Conservative government had won that round and successfully put pressure on people in order to stop the Sunday Pictorial publishing the whole story

For the Conservative government, the dam was going to burst at any time, and they knew it. Can you imagine how those senior Conservative ministers from Macmillan downwards must have driven themselves mad, day and night, trying to stop the flood gates from bursting open, just because Profumo had got his dick out and fucked Keeler?

Oh boy! I've heard of some fucks in my time, but that was one expensive fuck!

Obviously there were deals being done with everybody: court officials, judges.

How the fuck could they delay the case over a min-cab driver?

On March the 8th Keeler disobeyed court orders to appear as witness against me and ran to hide in Spain.

Theoretically this would be a guarantee to delay my trail even further which was yet another bonus for the Conservative party who were still desperate to keep it all quiet.

Any defence counsel in the world now could have got me an adjournment with the principal witness on the missing list, but with me safely locked away at the Psycho Ward, the plot thickened.

Deals were being done and my defence counsel threw me to the wolves.

CHAPTER 14
MY TRIAL AT THE OLD BAILEY

On the morning of March the 15th, I was woken early, as is the custom when a prisoner has to make an appearance in court. As we were put in the meat wagon, one of the warders reading his sheet said,

"We've got an attempted murder charge in the number one court at the Old Bailey. That's a big one," he carried on.

Realising it was me whom he was talking about; the prison officer gave me a very funny look, as he locked me in the little portable cell inside the prison van. That transport van drops fifteen-odd prisoners off at the various parts of London, to all the different courts. Making all those stops, you're locked up in that small space driving round London for quite a long time. There's only just enough room to sit down inside your own locked compartment, and stare out of the frosted window at normal life, on the street outside. I was in a world of my own. In less than an hour's time, I was being delivered to the jury of twelve strangers. These men and women, whom I had never met, would then decide my fate. On the way to the court I was worried, but not overly so, because my solicitor Irvin Shaw, had repeatedly told me that the maximum I would get would be, six to nine months. I had already done three months, so theoretically I could be out in another ten weeks. At the absolute worst, I would be free by Christmas. The Prison van arrived at the Old Bailey and I was taken out and put in the cells under the actual courts. I had been sat there for what seemed liked hours when suddenly the door flew opened and the court official shouted,

"Edgecombe. You're in now."

The officer led me up a steep flight of narrow stairs, and I suddenly found myself standing in the dock of the famous Number One Court. The place was packed.

The Number One Court at the Old Bailey is an awe inspiring place at the best of times, but for a black prisoner in the dock, now facing an all white jury, it was the big one. I looked round the court to try to find another black face, but all I could see staring back at me was a sea of white faces. This wasn't to be John Edgecombe's day.

I was the main attraction, and newspapers all over the country had waited for this for months. It was as if all the reporters from the public gallery were shouting,

"Thanks Johnny Boy. You shot the shots, now let's hear the stories. Give us the dirt!"

I remember that the jury looked very serious. It was as if they were all looking at me, expecting me to suddenly pull a gun from my pocket and shoot them all.

I looked around the court for the familiar face of my solicitor Irwin Shaw, but he wasn't there. I couldn't see him anywhere. In his place was another solicitor, a total stranger. It was a barrister called Moles. I don't know why, but at that moment, for the first time, my heart started beating faster. I knew something was going wrong for me big time.

Up until then, my case had hardly been mentioned in the newspapers and not wanting to face reality I still kidded myself that my only real crime was damaging a door and possessing a gun. I think what made me realize that I was in at the deep end, was standing in the dock. It suddenly dawned on me where I actually was. This wasn't a local Magistrates Court. I was in the Old Bailey, where they tried the most serious cases, and gave out severe sentences.

My trial started and I now found myself doing legal battle with Griffiths Jones the prosecuting barrister. Jones was a top man who later himself became a Judge. The case opened with the prosecution stating that the key witness, who had deferred charges against me, was not in court. Therefore there was no one there to say I had shot a gun at them. The case should have stopped there and then, but the prosecuting counsel assured the court he had enough evidence to continue in her absence. Hearing that Keeler was not in court my spirits lifted, but only for a brief moment. The charges against me were now were being reduced from attempted murder to possession of a firearm with intent to endanger life. I was confused, because with no witness to say I shot at her, there was no case to hear. But the case was still going ahead.

Where was my solicitor?

Where was my barrister?

Why weren't they stopping the case?

Things then went from bad to worse, when my so-called barrister got up and spoke. His words were very damaging:

"I can assure this court my client had nothing whatsoever to do with the disappearance of the key witness, Christine Keeler. When Keeler vanished my client was in custody at the time."

What the fuck was the jury going to think now?

One minute they are being told about a black man with a gun trying to murder Keeler, and in the next breath they were being told that Keeler was missing altogether.

What were they going to assume? Keeler was dead and that I had arranged it all!

Under these circumstances, did my defence ask for an adjournment until the witness was found and brought into Court for my cross-examination?

Hell no!

What they did do was a deal with the prosecution to give the green light to let my case go ahead.

Handcuffed in the dock, I now looked like a contract killer who had got rid of the key witness. I wanted to scream but the words wouldn't come out. I was frozen to the spot, my life in the hands of other people.

That day two incidental witnesses were called: the first, Mandy Rice-Davis, who said exactly what she saw

happen, which was me shooting at a door. She
categorically denied ever seeing me shoot at the missing
witness, Christine Keeler. Then, the mini-cab driver was
called, but he had seen nothing except me shooting at a
door. These two people, Mandy and the Mini-Cab driver,
were the only people called by the court, apart from
numerous forensic police officers who only gave lengthy
evidence about finding bullets embedded in a front door.

The prosecuting barrister cross-examined me without
mercy, indicating all types of innuendos to the court. The
character he painted was that I was a hardened gunman,
possibly a contract killer. All the time I was looking
round, and wondering why my barrister wasn't objecting
and helping me.

Before, or during my case I never spoke a single word to
my barrister or the new solicitor. The second day, of my
trial, was used for Lucky Gordon to give evidence against
me. Lucky's evidence was quite weak. He said that there
was a whole mob of people fighting, and therefore it was
impossible to prove that it was me that actually cut him.

At that stage I naively still believed that on the charge of
attempted murder, I would be found not guilty. There was
still a part of me that thought I would be going home that
night.

To stand in the dock in the Number One Court, with all
of that going on, is a horrifying ordeal. Everything about
my case was a fit-up. The charges were juggled about to
ensure that the jury brought back a guilty verdict, on a
charge where I could be sent down for a long time.

When you're charged with murder, or attempted murder, legally it's broken up into three counts,

The first count is 'attempted murder'.

The second is 'possessing a gun with intent to endanger life'.

The third is 'possessing a fire arm without a license'

At the end of the case, the judge instructed the jury not to bring in any verdict on the third count, because that carried a maximum of two years. By having no verdict on the last count the jury only had to decide, guilty or not guilty on the first two counts. These were the judge's instructions.

The Judge whose name was Mr Justice Thesiger summed up the case by saying,

"In the old days in Wimpole Mews, a black man would have only been there clearing up the horse shit as a footman."

With instructions not to bring in a verdict on the last count the jury were forced to bring in a verdict on the first two of attempted murder or possessing a firearm, with the intent to endanger life. The jury could not possibly find me guilty of attempted murder because there was nobody there in court to claim I had attempted to murder them. This left the jury with one option only: bring in a guilty or not guilty verdict on a charge of possessing a firearm with the intention of endangering life. The jury were told not to split this second charge in two, and therefore had no choice but to find me guilty or not guilty on both parts of the charge.

No judge can tell the jury to find the defendant guilty, but what that judge did was inexcusable.

On the first half of the only charge left I was obviously guilty. I had possessed a firearm and by linking the two the jury were forced in to returning a guilty verdict on the second part too, this being the intent to endanger life.

Who did this to me? I accuse the whole establishment of protecting the English way of life. Not everybody, however, was prepared to play ball and go along with this farce. Some people still had principles, like Marcus Lipton, the Labour MP for Brixton who the following day, wrote a letter to The Guardian newspaper in my defence.

With the judge's summary over, the jury retired and I was taken down to the cell. It seemed like I had just sat down when I was being taken back up to court to hear their verdict.

I looked at the jury, and even they didn't seem that bothered. I think most of them just thought that I was going to get six to nine months. After all, what I had done was actually not that serious.

When you are summoned for jury service you have to go. Those twelve people were there because they had to be there. They were not legal experts but that day in court they all had been given very precise instructions by the judge, which they followed. I don't think any of them expected me to get a long sentence.

The clerk of the court turned to the jury and said,

"How do you find the defendant John Edgecombe, guilty or not guilty?"

The foreman of the jury stood up and announced,

"We find the defendant guilty of possessing a firearm with intent to endanger a life."

The Judge now, with stern eyes, looked at me. What he should have said was,

"Before I pass sentence do you have anything to say?"

This is customary in every case before sentencing. It's a formal procedure to give the accused a last chance to plead for lenience in his sentence. This plea could be as simple as saying sorry, or the accused could even give mitigating circumstances as to why he or she committed the crime in the first place.

Instead the Judge just said,

"Seven years!"

Seven years!

I stood there and heard the words "seven years" over and over again. I held on to the dock, I was shaking. Seven years, those words rang round the court. "Seven years, seven years."

I looked up at the Judge, in his wig, and all his fancy court attire with the sword, hanging on the wall behind his head. I wanted to jump up and become Judge, Jury and Executioner myself, grab the sword and cut the fucker's head off.

By this time, my barrister seemed to have completely vanished. That bastard. His job had been done, and I had been put down for seven years. In the dock, I had been handcuffed throughout the trial, and I was now led back down to the cells like some big-time criminal. It was like I was an international hit man, employed by the President of the United States, to keep Christine Keeler's sexual activities with him secret. The court jailers in charge below were actually quite sympathetic. They were all shocked too.

"Seven years," said one of them. "That's impossible!"

At that time, the screws obviously didn't have a clue as to what really was going on and the conspiracy behind it all.

What they could see though was that there was far more to it than met the eye for me to be given seven years when I should only have got six months.

In the cell under the courts was another prisoner who had just been sentenced. He had received twenty-one years for armed robbery. Somehow, in a perverse kind of way, hearing this made me feel better.

An hour or so later, the meat wagon was ready to take us back to prison. Outside the court it was mobbed with cameramen. They were all trying to get a photograph but with me hidden inside they couldn't get proper pictures. Instead of taking us to Brixton, we were both taken to Wandsworth Prison to begin our sentences.

The Christine Keeler show had officially opened, and now the first act was being played out for the British public to gossip about over their breakfasts the following morning.

The whole world loves a scandal, and as scandals go, there's nothing better than a sex scandal involving an important, respectable government minister getting inside the knickers of an eighteen-year-old girl. Add a Russian spy, the President of America, and two black men smoking hash, and (as all the newspaper editors knew that day, rubbing their hands) you have got a story, and a good one, a story that would sell a lot of newspapers.

Me, I had served my purpose in shooting my gun. I had now been conveniently sentenced, and locked-up, out of the way, where nobody would take any notice of me, or believe any of the things I knew.

On the day I was sentenced I was devastated, but in many ways, as I look back today, I should count myself lucky. The conspirators had just made sure that I was locked away.

Stephen Ward, like many others, was actually killed to ensure his silence.

CHAPTER 15
SEVEN PRISON YEARS BEGIN

During those first few days in prison I could not think straight. I was in shock and totally numb. The only thing that span round in my head was that I was to be there for seven years. Seven years is a fucking long time.

I tried to visualize what those seven years were going to be like.

Imagine sitting in your lounge for seven years, without ever going out of that room.

That's a long, long time in your lounge. Back in those days, big-time bank robbers were getting seven or eight years, and now the establishment had thrown me into that same category.

In court, like all prisoners not yet found guilty, I was allowed to wear my own clothes. I had been wearing a mohair suit and looked quite dapper. During that time in my own clothes I still felt, to some degree, normal but in Wandsworth Prison, all that was to quickly change.

On arriving at the prison, I was led into the reception ward where, before being interviewed, I was handed my prison clothes. Along with my prison uniform I was given the standard prison kit, which consisted of; a shit-pot, a knife, fork and spoon and a tin mug. I was also given: one grey blanket and a sheet, a razor without a blade, a shaving brush and a bit of soap. That was my lot.

Here I stood, dressed in that drab, grey prison suit, clutching my gear, with seven years ahead of me.

Due to the nature of my sentence, I was immediately put on Rule 36. This is when they lock you up for twenty-three and a half hours a day - every day.

For the remaining half an hour a day, you are taken into a small exercise yard, where you walk round and round in a circle, like circus animals. I was classified as a dangerous prisoner and therefore had a cell to myself. In those days anyhow, they were not going to put a black and white guy in a cell together. Even in prisons, racism was bad - real bad.

The following day in The Daily Mirror, Marcus Lipton was again protesting on my behalf, saying that this was a deviation from the normal practice of British justice. On the outside all hell had broken loose. The newspapers were now having a field day. Suddenly, I was the celebrity prisoner in the middle of Britain's latest scandal. In fact, this was the first decent scandal since Lady Chatterley's lover. It was all happening for so many people. Christine Keeler's failure to appear in court came before Mr. Justice Liars at the Old Bailey. Marcus Lipton asked the attorney general how many crown witnesses had not shown up. Barbara Castle had also become involved.

Three days later, the News of the World published Stephen Ward's story. I never read it but I guess Stephen Ward was feeling safer with me inside. He probably still believed he could avoid the espionage charges. Both governments knew there was about to be a scandal exposed but neither really knew what was going to happen as a result of it. A day after that Mandy Rice –Davis' story was to appear in the Daily Sketch. The following day George Wig openly asked in parliament, as to who actually had slept with Keeler.

On March the 22nd, Profumo officially denied in parliament, that he had ever had sex with Keeler. The next morning, every newspaper in the country carried Profumo's denial, although most editors didn't believe it. I read the newspaper in prison and thought, "Oh boy it must have been your identical twin brother bouncing up and down on the bed."

Two days later, the key witness in my trial, the precious Christine Keeler, appeared at a police station in Madrid and told her story to the Daily Express. The following day they ran the Christine Keeler story.

Locked away in my cell I especially did not read the papers. It all upset me too much because I knew now Christine Keeler had just used me and sold me down the river. To be in love with a woman and then find you are serving seven years because of her is very disturbing, I felt devastated.

After reading their daily newspapers the prison officers on my wing now made me their subject of conversation. I don't know if it was what they read, or because I was black, but now they were all against me even more. Many of them now insisted on me calling them Sir.

One day I said to one of them.

"Who the fuck knighted you?"

I meant it as a bit of a joke, but it backfired on me. The following morning I was dragged before the Governor, and lost three days remission.

Commenting on my rude remark, the governor's words that day were:

"People like you should know your place in society."

The governor looked at me sternly, and said,

"You were told to come in to this prison and keep quiet. And if you want to serve your seven years peacefully, that is exactly what I advise you to do – keep quiet!"

I remembered the words of the Kray henchmen in the car by the 'All Nighters Club' that night and decided there and then, for my own safety, to keep quiet. For the next six weeks I remained on rule 36, after which I was transferred over to the main prison.

I was to stay in Wandsworth Prison for eighteen months.

Over in the main block I was taken before the duty psychiatrist, who told me to plead that I had an inferiority complex when I came up for my appeal. Inferiority complex? I didn't exactly understand what the fuck he was talking about, but perhaps he meant well.

Next to come into my prison life was the Catholic priest, who laid into me in a very hostile way.

"You deserve exactly what you've received. You should have been given a longer sentence longer or even been hanged." He had obviously had a word with God earlier that day.

My appeal was due to be heard quite soon. At that time Barbara Castle was demanding my release and re-trial, and was constantly asking Henry Brooks why this couldn't happen. Harold Wilson, at his speech in Scarborough, also indicated that he wanted my re-trail. I was sure he did. After all, it was him that set up the whole fucking deal. Another MP, Alison Bacon, was demanding that they discuss my case in the House of Commons. There were so many devious things going on. I am sure with many politicians their right hand didn't know what the left was doing.

Numerous people in the Labour party were now putting pressure on the Prime Minister, Harold Macmillan, to give me a re-trial. I realise now that these bastards weren't actually interested in my re-trial. They weren't campaigning for Johnny Edgecombe to be walking free down the Portobello road, smoking another joint. What they were interested in was to keep the story alive and bring down the Conservative government. I would like to ask Barbara Castle why, when a few months later, the Labour government were in power, they then did absolutely nothing to help me. When the Conservatives were in charge the Labour government kept demanding my re-trial, but as soon as they, themselves, were in power they forgot all about me.

I felt very bitter at being their scapegoat.

Sitting there hopeless in prison, I was caught between two governments. Macmillan wanted to keep me locked away to protect his hierarchy, whereas Harold Wilson was trying to win the election and get into power. He wanted me back in court so they could carry on exposing everybody. At least that's how it was before Labour got into power.

For three months while I was in prison awaiting my appeal, I received repeat visits from Irvin Shaw. In spite of my anger over having been sentenced to seven years, Irvin Shaw somehow convinced me that we would definitely get the whole thing reduced on appeal. Some days I actually began to believe we had a chance and I would go free.

While locked up, a prisoner mentally clings on to every last hope of release, and this is exactly what I was doing before each visit. I was just kidding myself, though, because it was always the same. Each visit began with the usual sickly smile accompanied by the words,

"Hello how are you John? Here's a cigarette."

Then quickly we got onto the usual questions. We only ever talked about the sex life of Christine Keeler. Irvin Shaw wanted to know what drugs Christine took, whom she had slept with, and if I had I actually seen her in bed with President Kennedy. He wanted all the dirt.

Some time later most of what I told him appeared in both Italian and French newspapers. I'll always remember what he said as he left at the end of each visit.

"John don't ever write to me about all these sex stories because with your appeal pending it could jeopardize everything."

My appeal came up sometime in June, and in court I had to deal with the Head of Justice, Charlie Parker, who didn't really have a lot to say. With a sickly grin on his face his words simply were,

"The maximum sentence for endangering life is fourteen years. You only got half, consider yourself lucky. Go back to prison, serve your seven years, and just keep quiet."

"Keep quiet, keep quiet!"

The whole fucking world was telling John Edgecombe to keep quiet.

The entire appeal hearing was a fiasco, and everything was thrown out of court. With my last chance now gone, I had seven lonely years in front of me.

I soon found myself, once more, sitting alone, back in my cell in Wandsworth Prison.

Looking back now, I realise that even if I had gone to Wimpole Mews with a water pistol, I'd have still been charged with attempted murder.

I was a small pawn in a big game of chess, where not only the British government was at stake, but the rumours had also rocked President Kennedy and the White House in America.

Back in prison, the harsh reality soon set in. I was now totally on my own. Nobody was ever going to listen to me until I was a free man. Anything I had to say would now have looked like an attempt to get myself out of prison. It's hard to describe how I now felt towards Keeler but sitting there with seven years in front of me I felt like a trapped fox caged in. My spirit, however, was not completely dead and I now started writing to the home office with my own petitions. They never replied.

CHAPTER 16
A VISIT TO LORD DENNING

A month or so later I had a big surprise. Very early in the morning my cell door burst open. A prison officer that I had never seen before was standing there with my civilian clothes.

"What's happening?" I asked.

"You're going out for the day," he said sarcastically. "You're going to Downing Street."

Going to Downing Street? What was a black man like me going to Downing Street for? I sure as hell was not going for a tea party. I got changed into my civilian clothes and was ready to go, when the officer told me to sit down.

"Listen carefully, Edgecombe. You are serving seven years, and there's two ways of serving your sentence. There's the easy way, where you get your food everyday, your allowance, and you can sleep safely in your bunk at night, without fear of any accidents happening. Or, Edgecombe, there is the hard way where accidents happen. In my time as a prison officer, I have seen horrible accidents with prisoners thrown over the landing, or found battered to death in their cells, and I do not want to see this happen to you. Spreading malicious rumours about people on the outside can only cause you problems, especially when you're locked up in prison. In half an hour, two of my officers are going to take you to see Lord Denning at Downing Street. Lord Denning wants to speak to you and put his mind at rest that you haven't got any damaging rumours."

It was like a scene from the Godfather, but I wasn't watching it on the screen. This was my real life in Wandsworth Prison. Then, dressed in my civilian clothes, I was led to the prison gate, where a large Rolls-Royce type car was waiting. Inside the car sat another man, with a long scar down the side of his face.

It was Lucky Gordon.

"What the fuck," I thought to myself,

"Why were two black cats like us going on a ride to Downing Street?"

Lucky and I didn't speak a word. We just sat there, handcuffed to our prison officers, staring at each other.

Here was the man with the scar down his face, that had caused me all this trouble in the first place, and now we were going for a cosy little ride together, to talk with Lord Denning.

In reality Lord Denning was preparing a report on behalf of Macmillan, as a last attempt to keep the Conservative government in power.

This was the sixty's madness at its very best. Macmillan hoped the Denning report would save his government but it was too late to camouflage and hide his minister's sex habits.

"Fuck it," I thought to myself. "I've been sold down the river. I have got nothing to lose. I am going to rot for seven years in prison, so I am going to tell Lord Denning everything." Believe me, I had plenty, and the evidence to back it up.

The photographers and newsmen obviously knew about our visit way in advance, because mopeds and cars chased us all the way. There were photographers everywhere. We were like two black pop stars, arriving for a concert. Handcuffed to our prison officers, we were driven into a locked courtyard, which stopped the photographers coming any further. Inside the building the two of us were taken to a large room and told to wait.

"You're first, Edgecombe." With that, I stood up and was taken into a very large office where Lord Denning was seated at the far end, behind a very big desk. I wasn't really sure why we were there in the first place, and in my naive mind, I thought that this was some new appeal on my behalf. Why else would they take us out of prison?

Denning spoke.

He looked down at me and said, in a very matter of fact way.

"John Edgecombe, when I have finished talking to you, you are going back to prison where you will be kept locked up for another seven years. Behave yourself, and nothing worse than that will happen to you. Misbehave yourself by spreading untrue or malicious rumours, and I cannot be responsible for what happens to you." His speech continued, sounding like a tape recording of the prison officer earlier that morning in my cell saying, "There are two ways to serve your sentence," blah, blah, blah.

Lord Denning repeated the prison officer's repertoire practically word for word. I knew exactly what Denning meant. I could almost picture myself being thrown over the landing, from three flights up and my dead body smashed to pieces on the prison floor.

Believe me, in prison there are some hard fuckers serving twenty years with nothing to lose. For an extra ounce of tobacco they would do anything. On top of that, there were always screws that would turn their back while a black man was thrown over the railings from three floors up.

Lord Denning looked straight at me, and I will never forget his final words,

"John Edgecombe, I am relieved you haven't got any malicious rumours. It's better for you that way, isn't it?"

He was smiling, and even I smiled now, due to the relief of knowing I wasn't going to be executed.

"Yes," I replied.

I now had a weird feeling, like I wanted to hug him. It was as if we had finally settled an issue once and for all.

I was taken outside and now it was Lucky Gordon's turn to be interviewed.

A short while later, Lucky and I were driven back to Wandsworth prison. Again, during the journey we didn't speak, but Lucky had a funny look on his face, as if he knew what was about to happen. I couldn't stop staring at his scar. It was very tense. You could feel the hatred between us.

Two weeks later Lucky Gordon's appeal was heard, granted, and he was released. He was now a free man.

With Lucky released they could now automatically charge Christine Keeler with perjury. It was solely on the evidence of Keeler that Lucky was convicted. They now bought Christine to court, where she was sentenced to six months in Holloway. This was just another Conservative move on the political chessboard. The idea behind it was that when she came out of prison, whatever she said would be discredited.

Through the establishment's need to discredit Christine Keeler, Lucky that day really was lucky.

CHAPTER 17
STEPHEN WARD

When I was first sentenced I still had a lot of fight in me but as the days and weeks turned to months my spirit started to sag. Any hope had vanished. With my appeal turned down a kind of depressive acceptance set in. There now was absolutely nothing I could do except sit in prison. Slowly I began to accept my situation.

Meanwhile on the outside the heat was on for other people. The News of the World printed the Keeler story, and shortly after Stephen Ward was arrested. When I heard Stephen was arrested I felt sorry for him. I didn't know why he'd been arrested and even when I was handed a newspaper I couldn't follow what was going on. I wrote a letter to Stephen Ward, encouraging him not to let the motherfuckers get him down. I didn't mention our conversations because I thought that would only make more trouble and I could somehow get an even longer sentence – perhaps fourteen years. Sitting in my cell I began to feel fortunate, almost like I had been given a reprieve.

At least I was alive. I had a premonition as to what was about to happen to Stephen Ward.

The next day I was called out of my cell and taken to the interview room. Waiting for me there, were the police. The Governor warned me that I didn't have to talk to the police if I didn't want to. I didn't know what they wanted but hoping it might benefit me, I agreed to meet them.

I sat down in front of these two really evil looking bastards, who said to me,
"We've come to ask you some questions about Stephen Ward."

To which my reply was, "The two of you can fuck off. You're wasting your time."

I was then taken out of the room and went straight back to my cell. Alone and back in my cell, I realised that although I was serving seven years I was probably a damn sight better off than Stephen Ward! The same people who had destroyed me, the same system, the same establishment, was now about to destroy Stephen.

Somehow I knew it was Stephen's turn, and he was going to get worse than me. In my letter to Stephen I had told him not to let it all get him down. All wasn't lost, and even if they sent him down, he was a great artist and could develop his talent in prison.

Trying to encourage him, I suggested that he could redeem himself, and re-invent himself in prison as a famous portrait painter. I also wrote that I was sorry for shooting at his front door. I am sure he understood exactly what I really meant!

Stephen did receive my letter and a copy of it was printed in The Guardian newspaper. I don't know how close it all got to Stephen actually being charged with espionage and him going to prison for forty years. Perhaps it was all about to happen. It was however too late.

A day later Stephen Ward was dead.

CHAPTER 18
STEPHEN WARD DIES

When the news came through that Stephen Ward was dead, I wasn't even surprised that the newspaper had said it was suicide, but I knew who had pushed the button on that one, and there was little I could do about it.

In a way when Stephen Ward died so did my involvement in the whole Profumo scandal. I'd been of use and was now left to rot in prison while everybody else including Keeler got on with their lives and just forgot all about me.

I don't remember exactly when, but some time later, the Labour government got into power. When I heard the news I was excited and loads of prisoners came to my cell in celebration. They all had optimistic ideas.

"You'll get a retrial now, possibly a pardon now Wilson is Prime Minister," they all cried out.

Some of the prison officers thought the same and one laughed saying,

"Don't get too comfortable. You're going home soon"

The Labour party had made such a big effort to re-try my case, and they were now in government. They were now firmly in the legal position to do whatever they wanted. I waited expecting my cell door to open with good news but how wrong was I to be.

Harold Wilson turned out really to be a wolf in sheep's clothing. As Prime Minister he had the automatic right to give me a re-trial, or even a pardon. What did he, or his 'Annie Oakley' sidekick, Barbara Castle do?

Sweet fuck all.

I was left to rot.

Harold Wilson is dead now, but Barbara Castle, I challenge you today to come forward while you're still living and put the record straight. Tell the world how you used, and then abused me by not helping me.

I remained in Wandsworth Prison until August 1964. During my whole stay there I was kept in a cell by myself, because anybody who had been done for violence and been given a long sentence, was always kept alone. I was now very bitter and very resentful.

CHAPTER 19
GREAT TRAIN ROBBERY

It was August the 8th 1963. Whichever gang of politicians in high places actually wanted to put a stop to all of this media publicity now found a way.

Perhaps, it was all started in Scotland by some official putting an extra load of used bank notes on the mail train to be taken down to London to be burnt. Anyway, the extra million pounds, definitely tempted Bruce Reynolds and his gang to bring their robbery forward a week or so.

To the relief of many senior government officials, on August the 8th 1963, the evening papers, at last carried a different type of headline.

Two-and-a-half million pounds had been stolen from a mail train at Sears Crossing in Buckinghamshire. The Train Robbers did what nobody else had been able to do, and finally put the Keeler scandal to bed.

The Beatles were singing 'Love me do'. The Train Robbers were counting their money, hiding in Acapulco or already doing time. Cassius Clay had knocked out Sonny Liston and become Mohammed Ali.

Fuck knows what Christine Keeler was up to, but I was alone in my cell with nobody replying to my petitions.

CHAPTER 20
WANDSWORTH PRISON

As time passed, I desperately tried to adapt to prison and set my own rules, which were to keep my eyes peeled, my nose clean, and my mouth shut. I was like a fish out of water because in prison, most other prisoners have already done quite long sentences before, in either approved schools or borstals. Most of my fellow convicts already had up to fifteen previous convictions. They were already totally institutionalised.

In the early days in prison I got various cryptic messages from the outside. To some degree my case was still talked about but as time went on that all changed. The political scene outside had moved dramatically and John Edgecombe like the whole Keeler Profumo affair was old news. I was locked up in prison and that's where I was going to stay so I gritted my teeth and made up my mind to do my best and get on with it. You can lock up a man's body but you can't lock up his mind.

Life went on, even though I was physically locked in prison, I refused to do the time mentally. To distance myself from it all I started to read a lot of Howard Robbins and Plato books, which enabled me to distract myself from the day-to-day environment of prison life.

Prison was not beneficial and I did not agree with the way it was being run. All my life I had been a hustler, I was not a hardened criminal, and in theory, after I had served my seven years there would be little chance of me getting involved in a major crime to serve another seven years.

Admittedly, prison is for people who have committed a crime, but surely the idea is to reform and rehabilitate them so that when they get out of prison, they don't continue to commit more crimes.

With the prison system as it was then and is still today, they defeat their object. Instead of rehabilitating prisoners, re-educating their thinking patterns, all the system does is humiliate them. Prison makes them sub-human and degrades them under filthy conditions. In a cell a man is given a shit-pot and has to go to the toilet in front of the other two prisoners who share his cell. How do you think it feels to have two people watching you take a shit? This loss of dignity just adds to the bitterness and hatred the prisoner has, not only for the prison authorities, but also for society in general.

If you hate society, you want to rebel against it, and the most natural way to rebel is to break the law.

Naughty boys aged ten break windows, naughty boys aged fifteen snatch handbags and naughty boys aged twenty commit robberies. When you catch them, you have to punish them, but that punishment should be geared towards rehabilitation so they do not repeat the same behaviour. Surely the idea should be to make the offender understand he would be better off doing an honest day's work. Instead of this, the prison system really degrades, humiliates and crushes the prisoner's self-esteem. Convicts are treated like the vermin of society. All that you accomplish is that you release the prisoners with such bitterness against society, that they commit crimes again, almost as soon as they get out.

In prison the routine was always the same. I was woken each day at six o'clock to slop-out. Slopping-out is when you put all you're shit and piss in a long troth, together with about fifty other lots of shit and piss from all the other prisoners. It is degrading. All this is done in a very crowded small space, and with a lot of pushing and shoving, piss is often spilt. No wonder prisoners fight with each other. You'd fight with your neighbour if you had to go to the toilet in this fashion.

"You fucking cunt you spilt piss on my trousers. I'll knife you, you fucker!"

"You fucking talk to me like that and I'll throw you over the landing."

That was the start of my day. Those were the typical conversations I would have to listen to at six-o'clock in the morning. At slop-out, peace, love and meditation was impossible for me, especially without a joint.

Then it was time to wash and shave. I don't know why everything is done in such a hurry in prison. It is madness because we are staying there all day anyway.

Now it was time for prison breakfast. We were made to stand and wait at the door of the cells for breakfast to come around.

Breakfast was served. Two guys came by. One slops tea in your mug, usually managing to spill it all over you, the other wallops a lump of solid porridge, which looks more like cement, on your plate. Holding out your dish was being like Oliver Twist in the Charles Dicken's novel.

After breakfast, which you ate in your cell, it was time for exercise. Everyday I was hounded into a small yard, where I had to walk around in circles, like a circus animal, for half-an-hour. Exercise over, it was then time for work. I was then taken to another part of the prison, to do the job I had been allocated.

I worked on a machine in the tailor shop, where I spent most of my time making exercise shorts for the army. The pay was five pence per week.

While you were working you were allowed to talk with your fellow workmates, but when work officially ended, it was totally different. Still sitting in the same place at the same workbench, while we waited to be told to stand up and queue for dinner, we were not allowed to talk - not a word. Imagine it, grown men sitting there for what could be five to ten minutes, and not even being allowed to say,

"Wonder what's for dinner today."

Talking was not allowed. And if you did pass the time of day, by perhaps saying something innocent like, "Any visits this week?" you would get nicked and lose three days remission.

It seemed to me that the prison regime was designed specifically to breed resentment, and I understand that it is still exactly the same today.

When our lunch call came, we walked in silence like zombies to the ground floor, where we would line up with other hungry prisoners waiting for their dinner. The food was disgusting and we carried our lunch up numerous flights of stairs and ate it in our cells.

After lunch it was circus time again, round and round the prison yard, for half an hour's exercise. Then, again like animals, we were lead back to the workshops.

Locked up every night, I didn't see another living soul from 7pm until 6 o'clock the next morning.

Alone in my cell at night, all the hatred and the resentment came out big time. I lay in my bunk, grinding my teeth, making my list of the motherfuckers in the establishment that I was going to shoot dead with 'dumb-dumb' bullets. With a dumb dumb bullet you shoot the bastard in the stomach, and when the bullet hits them it explodes and spreads inside their stomach, blowing a hole in their back.

My list was never ending, including: Harold Wilson, the Judge Parker, and Denning, the bastard. There were so many more - the whole fucking lot of them. The list went on and on. When I had finished mentally shooting them, only then could I go to bed in peace. In my fantasies I used to make up my own stories of how I would kill them all. First of all I had to escape from prison. Then I had to find a gun. I would usually get this from the IRA. Then in the dark of night, I would hunt those fuckers down and shoot them one by one. On many occasions, when the list was about ten to twelve people, it kept me up half the night, but there was work to be done. Even though I got very little sleep, those motherfuckers got their come-uppance.

Often as the cell door flew open in the morning, my first thoughts were, "Fuck! Did I kill Harold Wilson last night?"

During those eighteen months I really thought about my life. Here I was, in the middle of the biggest political scandal of the century. Murder, blackmail, espionage, oh fuck man; I had never imagined that all of this would happen to me after leaving the small island of Antigua.

I have always believed that life is pre-destined anyhow, and that everything is already written in the scrolls. Whoever wrote those scrolls sure wrote a strange story for me.

The messages for me to be peaceful and keep quiet continued to come during those eighteen months. There are still many things I cannot write about even today, because I want to stay alive, and if you expose a scandal at a certain level, things are no different from the middle ages when you were taken to the tower and executed. The only difference now, is that they don't want the publicity, so you just go on the missing list.

Eighteen months went by, when one day I got my marching orders. The reason I was being moved was because I had now become a bloody nuisance. I had spent months forever petitioning, and with every petition I insisted that it be put on official record. The amount of extra paper work I was creating for Wandsworth prison was huge. Henry Brooks, the Home Secretary, got the brunt of my petitions. I also wrote to the Civil Liberties and Justice. There are organisations that helped the underdog. Sadly, both these charitable organizations seemed already well under the cosh. Perhaps they were already under strict orders to tell me that my case had embarrassed the government enough and that I should just shut up and do my time.

Anyhow, Wandsworth prison and the higher authorities had by now, had enough of me. They needed to shift me to a quiet prison, out of the way of the prying eyes of the Press.

CHAPTER 21
DARTMOOR PRISON

What better place to send me than Devon, unfortunately not to a holiday camp, but to none other than Dartmoor prison.

When the screw came in to my cell and told me I was going to Dartmoor I was totally shocked. Dartmoor was reserved for big time criminals, spies, mass murderers or top bank robbers doing twenty-years. The authorities were now moving me up a league.

The ride to Dartmoor prison was a long journey, so we had to stop off half way at another smaller prison, where I spent the night. The following morning, after another long drive, we arrived at the new prison.

Arriving at Dartmoor was like something in a Sherlock Holmes film. That morning it was very misty, and as we approached, I could see this enormous gothic building in front of me. It looked very mysterious, and at that point I knew I was going to be living with long term, hard case prisoners.

"What are these prisoners going to be like?" I wondered. "Am I going to share a cell with a murderer?"

Upon arrival I was allocated to a cell, in the condemned wing. That condemned wing in part of this old prison should have been demolished years ago. It was a health hazard and so damp that prisoners could actually take in ginger snap biscuits, and by the following morning those rock hard biscuits would have gone soggy.

In the condemned wing you woke up to find your clothes were damp, your brain was damp, and even your soul became damp. It was like living in a broken sauna. A day later I was taken out of that humid hellhole to be put in another wing. There I met the Governor, an Irish man named Dennis Malone. The conversation went something like this. A screw stood in front of the Governor who was sat behind an enormous desk. The screw would say,

"Tell the Governor your name and number."

"Edgecombe. 846830"

The Governor then delivered the following speech. It was just like all the other 'keep quiet speeches' I had heard, which basically said if I remained quiet I would live, and if I opened my mouth I would be killed. The prison Governor, however, had a much more subtle way of putting this message across, but I understood his message loud and clear. I was led back to my cell, and I knew that my time in Dartmoor prison was not going to be easy.

First I was first put in A-wing where the convicts either side of me were evil looking bastards. In Wandsworth, I had already lost two weeks remission, and I had definitely decided that I was not going to lose any more. However this wasn't as easy as it looked. In spite of my super good behaviour, within a couple of weeks a screw confronted me over something trivial. I said absolutely nothing, but just looked at him and imagined all the

things I like to say. In spite of my silence, I was done for
dumb insolence, and hauled in front of the Governor.
Here I tried to defend myself, saying,

"I never said a word."

To which the Governor replied,

"Don't say another word, Edgecombe. You are a
borderline case and the next word you say is going to put
you into deeper trouble."

From behind his enormous desk he continued,

"Anyway, this time I will dismiss this case, but I am
warning you not to come back to me again under the
same charge, otherwise you are in deep, deep shit."

I thought of asking whether I could ever look at a screw
again, but I thought better of it and decided to keep quiet.

After that event I was shifted to D-wing where I was to
meet the real boss of the prison.

Up until that time I thought Dennis Malone was the real
governor, but I was to discover otherwise. There was
only one governor in Dartmoor prison and that was a man
who moved from wing to wing as he fancied. This man
roamed from cell to cell, depending on his mood, and
strutted about the prison wearing an army combat jacket,
laying down the law. Occasionally he would glance at his
watch and make a comment to a prisoner or a prison
officer, both of whom would jump to attention. The
prison authority did not employ this man. He was

actually a prisoner named Frank Mitchell, otherwise
known as the 'Mad Axe Man'. At six foot five and nearly
the same measurement across, everybody-prisoners and
officers alike-were petrified of him.

Frank Mitchell was a problem that the prison authorities
could not solve. He was a giant of a man, with such
incredible strength he could, even handcuffed, lift up a
prison officer and throw him across the room. It was
physically impossible to even hold him down. If there
was trouble, it would take at least six screws to control
him, and many would get injured, possibly badly, in the
process.

Nobody could control Frank. Even his eventual
executioners, the Kray Twins, were unable to handle his
physical strength. So to the prison authorities, the only
answer was to do some type of deal with him. Dennis
Malone, the Governor, told Frank that he could do, as he
liked, as long as he kept peaceful. Frank had originally
been sent to prison for only eighteen months. His
behaviour during that first short sentence was so bad, that
with all the additional imprisonment he got, for hitting
prison officers, he was still locked up nineteen years
later, without a release date. In his own world, Frank
Mitchell was a legend. For all the other convicts there
were prison rules, but for Frank Mitchell there were none.

One day, Frank Mitchell stopped me outside his cell to
talk. While he was talking to me, I could smell booze on
his breath. He smiled and took me in his cell and asked
me if I wanted a drink. In his cell was an enormous bottle
of whisky.

"Drink I would rather have some dope!" I said.

Frank smiled saying,

"Some people on the outside are grateful you fired that gun and next week you'll get anything you want."

With that he walked me out the cell and sent me on my way.

Frank's power in that prison was unbelievable for example radios. Until you had served four years, you were not allowed to have a radio in Dartmoor. Frank Mitchell's control in the prison was so powerful, that you could ask if he would put your own radio down under his name. If he liked you enough he said, "yes," then if you were ever caught with a radio you could then tell the screw that the radio was Frank's, and all would be well. The conversation would then go something like this,

"Where did you get this radio from?"

"No, no, no, the radio's not mine. Its Frank Mitchell's."

"Oh, that's OK then," the prison officer would say and walk away. With Frank's approval you could own a black market radio, quite openly in the prison, before you were officially allowed to have one.

One day an Irish screw called Brofy went to switch the television off while Frank and a few other prisoners were still watching it. Association time was over and officially everybody should already have been back in their cells. The programme still had ten minutes to run, but Brofy switched off the television. Frank who was watching the TV shouted out,

"Switch the fucking telly back on, you cunt!"

The response from Brofy was immediate. What did he do, tell the prisoners to go to their cells? No way! Frank had spoken, so Brofy put the television back on, waited until the programme had finished, and then, getting Frank's nod of approval, finally switched it off.

A week or so later Frank gave me a lump of dope and smiling he said.

"You're gonna be comfortable here, Johnny and anything you need, you let me know."

The remainder of my stay in Dartmoor prison was very peaceful, and I could have anything I wanted, I just had to ask Frank, and I got it.

Two years later I was on the move again, and having said goodbye to Frank, I was driven under lock and key to the Verne, a softer prison. As we drove away I could see Dartmoor vanishing in the mist. I just hoped that I would never see that fucking place again.

CHAPTER 22
VERNE PRISON

My new prison, the Verne, was an ex-army camp situated in Dorset, and to get to it you had to go over a small bridge. Some days the weather was so windy that the screws had to tie a rope from the dormitory where the prisoners slept to the mess hall where they ate. At lunchtime it was quite a funny sight, with fifty or sixty prisoners, all desperately hanging onto a rope, trying to get to the mess hall.

It was while I was at the Verne that I discovered that my mum had died. It was actually three months after her death that I found out. I had not seen my mum for at least fifteen years. I had written to her when I first went to prison, and she replied to me. Her reply had brought me down mentally big time. In her letter she was really blaming the white people, saying what the white people had done it all to me. She had never wanted her fifteen-year-old boy to get on that ship in the first place and vanish into a strange land. She wanted me to grow up by the sea with people my own colour. Her letter might have been racist, but it was basically true.

My mum had never really left our small Caribbean Island and she saw it her way. To my mum I had always been caught between the devil and the deep blue sea. There I was in England, living with the white devils. The deep blue sea had separated me from her peaceful home in Antigua. After those few letters I had stopped communicating with my mum altogether. I felt there was nothing she could do for me, from her little Island of Antigua. She was in a helpless position and couldn't do anything to help me and I thought it better to not give her all my misery in the post.

My job in the prison was to put coal in the bunkers to heat the various outbuildings. Every day after finishing work, to avoid being given something else to do, I would skive, by hiding in the church bunker.

All incoming letters are read first by the authorities, and when there was bad news, such as a bereavement, they first give the letter to the priest who then would disclose the news. My cellmate knew of my movements and told the priest where he could find me.

The priest came in and said,

"Sit down John, I've got some bad news for you."

He did not have to say anything else because I knew what the news was.

The priest continued, "Your mother's dead."

My mum had died, and I was really sad, but for some reason I couldn't express my sadness.

In fact afterwards I felt guilty that I didn't feel sadder. I wasn't feeling the immense sense of loss that I should have done with my mum dying. I think this was because I had always been emotionally closer to my dad. It was him who had taken me away from my mum on those exciting sailing trips.

After the priest had told me the news, I returned to the dormitory where my fellow prisoner, a Burmese man, was more upset for me than I was over my mum's death.

Life continued in the Verne quite quietly. It's a different world from Dartmoor.

CHAPTER 23
THE HOSTEL

After serving six months in the Verne, I was transferred
to Pentonville prison. I was sent there to plead in front of
a committee, who would decide whether or not I could
now move to a hostel. A committee of four prison
officials, who, as usual, sat behind yet another an
enormous desk, took my interview. It was all extremely
intimidating. Your freedom is at stake, and you obviously
want to answer the questions in a favourable manor.
Believe me, those interviews are not so cut and dry. I
stood there nervously as one official spoke.

"Why do you want to go to a hostel?"

My reply was quite straightforward. I told them,

"I just want to put some bread together so that I can start
a new life in Africa."

One of the guys replied,

"Do you want to go to Africa to commit more crimes?"

I jumped up indignantly and started shouting,

"After all the crimes you guys have committed in Africa
you haven't left any other crimes for my imagination!"

There was silence. I just stood there realizing I should
have kept my mouth shut, but it was too late.

"Interview's over," one of the officials said.

That was it. Without another word I was led out of the room. I was refused a transfer to the hostel and sent back to the Verne.

Back at the Verne I told the Governor that I was going to send a petition to the home office, claiming racial discrimination. I did write another of my letters but as per usual got no reply. Sometime later, however, I was at last sent to a hostel in Walton, which was a part of a prison just outside Liverpool.

The arrangements at the hostel were as follows: during the day of course you were allowed out to go to work on the condition you returned by 6 pm each evening. You also paid a percentage of your wages to stay at the hostel. At weekends, provided someone with a clean record signed you out, you could sleep out all of Saturday night.

I was given the lousiest outside job out of everybody in the hostel. My job was cleaning off odd bits of concrete from the shuttering that were hired out to various building companies. It was a horrible job, on my own outside in the freezing cold all day.

The only good thing about the job was the boss. He was a nice white guy actually called Mr. White and he was originally from London. With me being from London too, he somehow took a liking to me.

On my first week he said to me, "The other guys here don't have to know you're from prison."

It didn't worry me at all because I had already told them where I was. I had no choice really. They all wanted to know where I was living and why I wouldn't go out for a drink with them in the evenings.

Racism was bad in those days. One weekend one of my fellow workers, JB, took me to a wedding reception. At the party we were standing six-deep at the bar, and a white guy pushed me out the way calling me,

"A black cunt."

I smiled and walked away, and then he repeated,

"You black cunt."

At this stage he forced his way back through the crowd and confronted me,

"Didn't you hear what I called you?"

I said, "Yeah, try something new man, 'cause I've been called all that so many times before."

At this he seemed to calm down, and asked me if I was a student. I told him that I was in prison and we got talking. After hearing my story he completely changed towards me and became quite sympathetic. He called one of his brothers over to meet me. His brother, however, came towards us, jaws and fists tightly clenched ready for war, thinking that a fight was about to happen. Then the guy quickly told him, "No, no, I want you to meet him. It's all cool." Anyhow things calmed down, we all got friendly and the brother even offered me a chick for the night.

Sadly I had to refuse, explaining I had to go back to prison because my curfew was up. And so life went on.

CHAPTER 24
FREEDOM

After about six months I was released from the hostel and found myself a free man, standing outside Liverpool prison with a little bit of money in my pocket. It was now 1967. During my first day of freedom I went to see a Jamaican guy in Parliament Street, in Liverpool, who had often signed me out for weekends. He was an all right guy. On that first day he gave me a smoke and fixed me up with a chick. I smoked the joint and did something else with the chick. I was with this chick for three or four day's non-stop. Through the sex and smoke I desperately tried to erase the memory of all those years in prison. But as much as I tried the scars wouldn't go away. I wanted to put it all behind me and become my old-self again, but I couldn't. Being in the prison had taken its toll. When I went into prison I was a happy-go-lucky guy, but when I was released, something inside me had gone and was gone forever. That something, whatever it was, never fully came back. The prison stigma was going to be with me forever.

A week later I left Liverpool for London.

I was thirty-five years old now, and when I arrived in London I went to see my buddies, Art Bloomfield and John Matthews. Art lived in Isleworth, and I stayed with him for a while. I was a free man, and yet in a strange way, with no newspapers running after me, I felt discarded. I had plenty to say but couldn't talk because nobody now wanted to hear anything. When I had gone into the prison at the beginning of the scandal, there was all that excitement with the Labour government trying to get in, Vassal the spy, Profumo, and so much more, but now it was all old news. Like yesterday's papers, I was of no more interest. The British justice system had betrayed me, and for the establishment I had served my purpose.

In London, at that time, I felt very vulnerable and desperate for cash; I went to see Irvin Shaw. I wanted my share of the money that he had been paid for the sex stories that appeared in foreign newspapers. Irvin Shaw insisted that he had not been paid any money from the papers, and therefore would not pay me. I looked at him and shook my head saying, "OK, OK I've been ripped off once again."

Things were not so good, and after the prison sentence I felt very low, so I decided to visit a guy I knew called Nose, who was a hustler who had moved from London to Birmingham. Like many convicts just released from prison, things were not so good money wise, so I took a job working at 'Lucas', the car accessory manufacturers. I worked the night shift, from 7pm until 7am. This was a long way from the limelight of the Christine Keeler era, and after two weeks there, I began to feel very disillusioned. I was so bored with it all, it was killing me mentally.

In that factory there was another man who had been working in that same bench for twenty years, and by now he was totally brain dead. I thought, "Oh fuck, I just got out of one prison and don't want to put myself into another, even if it is called Lucas." I gave my notice, and by using my two weeks wages, I put a deposit down and somehow got a loan to buy a little red MG sports car. Feeling a bit brighter I drove off down to the bright lights of London, to start off my second new life.

CHAPTER 25
MIKE TAYLOR

Back in London, my friend, John Matthews, had a mate called Bernie who owned a small boat, which was moored in Taggs Island, near Hampton Court. Bernie had apparently sold the boat to Tom, Dick and Mary, three smugglers from Manchester. The smugglers' main source of income was bringing in dope from Afghanistan. They had a scam that worked like this. With two different passports, (using only one) they boarded a flight from Manchester to Paris, changing at Heathrow. Flying to Heathrow from Manchester is an internal flight with no customs. Next, using the same passport you fly to Paris, and then with the other passport you leave the airport and hire a car and drive to Afghanistan. Here you would pick up the dope, and bring it back to Paris.

From Paris you could get through customs quite easily and you would then fly back into Heathrow, using the same passport, and fly on to Manchester in transit flights, avoiding customs altogether.

These three smugglers were extremely successful. Their profits soared, and they bought property everywhere. Everything went well at first and we all got on OK but after about a month I sensed that the smugglers were tired of me staying with them, I guess it was because I was smoking too much of their dope. We always smoked from a big cigar box, the sample box that contained the very best hash grown on planet earth. This special heavenly hash was only used for the would-be customers, who were sampling what they were about to buy. It's always been the same with hash dealers, because when you go to buy, they bring out the best for you to sample. They realized they couldn't get their shit together while I was around, so we mutually parted, and a week and a hundred joints later, I got a flat in a block called Garden Court in Hampton High Road. I moved in there, put my feet up, and rolled a joint.

The rent was quite expensive and I needed someone to share with me, so I spoke to my friend, Art, to see if he knew anyone. Art told me about a pianist he knew called Mike Taylor. At that time this chap, Mike Tailor, was really quite mad. His present residence was out in the open under the stars on Richmond Park. Art, who was friendly with Mike Taylor, was very concerned about his friend's mental health. He kept on at Mike, saying that he would get arthritis in his fingers and wouldn't be able to play the piano anymore if he carried on living in the park. Art brought Mike round to see me. We all had a chat and Mike moved in the same day. The first thing Mike did was roll a joint, and the second thing he did was buy a piano.

Mike Taylor was the pianist for the pop group Cream. The year was 1967 and they had just had great success in America. The group, Cream, were taking a break between tours and recording and Mike was chilling out. At the time Mike was not in the best of mental states. He had just split up with his wife after quite a dramatic division of property, which was as follows. Mike painted a black line down the middle of his flat, dividing each room in two, and his wife was under strict instructions not to cross over into his territory. Anyhow, as his personal life deteriorated, he moved from his pad to his new home under a tree in Richmond Park.

Hash smoking, drugging, plus heavy whiskey drinking had taken its toll on Mike. He had really crossed the borderline. He talked to himself constantly, swearing all the time. As my flat mate, he was lively to say the least. However, in a comical kind of way, he was really quite domesticated, and one afternoon I even found him ironing a pair of trousers. Slightly worse for wear, lifting the legs of the trousers in the air he yelled, "I'll cut your fucking head off!"

"That's not the head, Mike, it's the legs," I laughed back.

At which Mike laughed and took another swig from the whiskey bottle. Mike always cooked for himself at night, and it was always the same: eggs, bacon, sausage and beans. This was his idea of breakfast, but like the whole of his life, it was all out of tune eating breakfast at one in the morning. Every night in the early hours, from the kitchen, over and above the sizzling of the pan, came the nightly curses,

"Fuck off cunt! Fuck off!"

Then I would hear a crash as another plate or cup would be slammed to the ground. At first I replaced the broken china from Woolworths, but after a while the economics of the cutlery smashing was eating into his share of the rent, and I decided to go all plastic! Mike's response to the plastic cups and plates was quite indignant because it seemed to take away the drama of his, "Cunt-off–fuck-off!" out-bursts.

Over and above the madness, Mike was an amazing pianist, and often I would lay in bed for hours listening to him stroke the keys. We told each other our life stories and one night Mike offered to write me a song,

"It was all a scandal." he said, "You're black, we'll call it Black Scandal."

For days and days non-stop he worked on it, and one night he called to me,

"John come and listen to this."

He played me an amazing song, of which I still have the old cassette with the tune he played on the piano.

The other residents in our block of flats were mostly rich retired old ladies, who didn't really appreciate the piano playing or the 'cunt-off' ravings during the night. In spite of my efforts to keep the noise down with plastic plates, the complaints continued. I was told that the noise would have to be reduced or the police would be called.

Unfortunately, things went from bad to worse when Mike asked me to get him some speed tablets. I gave him some Benzedrine, and sadly after he swallowed the first few tablets, he started tripping all over again and went completely mad and started chopping up the piano keys. They were all over the floor. With the piano gone, he switched to the drum for a new kind of music. Mike now beat the drum all night long and this turned out to be the final straw for our neighbours. He cut up his clothes and ceremoniously gave me the 'Black Scandal' tape saying, "John, one day some day this will be a big, big hit. You wait and see Johnny boy." He then left and walked out of the flat. That was the last I saw of Mike Taylor.

A day or so later I had found out that Mike had visited a dealer called Tramp, leaving him some money for an ounce, but Mike disappeared without collecting his smoke. For several months no one saw him, then came bad news. His body was found washed up off Brighton Beach. The sex, drugs, and rock 'n' roll era of the sixties, had claimed yet another victim.

CHAPTER 26
MOROCCO

My Moroccan adventure, like every other adventure in my life, just seemed to happen. A new girl, Barbara, came into my life by chance. In a way, I had become like the black 'Forrest Gump.' Barbara had been married to a musician from New York. They had been recently divorced, and her family, who were extremely rich, had sent her to Ibiza to enable her to mentally get over her divorce problems. In Ibiza, with plenty of money to spend, a good time was being had by one and all. Barbara had bought a brand new Volvo and had had to come to England to collect it, because you cannot buy new Volvos so easily in Ibiza.

In England, Barbara met Harold MacNear, an established jazz musician, whom she had known from New York. Harold was a friend of mine, who often came to number 12 Lee Road to have a spliff. 12 Lee Road was the marijuana transit flat of central Europe. We were not dealers, but we had a supply of dope there at all times. "Peace and love man." The key was always in the front door, and those in the know just came in. There were dealers who popped in and out regularly - they had to. After all, if you're going to smoke that much hash, you have to buy it from somebody.

In those days we were classified as full-time hippies, and Barbara I suppose was what we called a weekend hippie. There were many weekend hippies in those days, people who wanted to drop out from society totally, but didn't have the courage to do so. Anyway, in her own way Barbara really did try to join the hippy clan, and would always take a puff on the passing spliff. Barbara was going to have her new Volvo, shipped back to Ibiza, when Harold came up with a good idea and suggested,

"Why don't you let Johnny drive the car back for you?"

She looked at me and said,

"Yeah, why not?"

So, two hours later there we were on the Dover to Calais ferry. Being with this rich chick Barbara, I had expected to stay in a top hotel and travel across France in style. Sadly, instead of luxury travel, Barbara had taken her hippie life a little bit too seriously, and we slept in the back of the car – without having any sex. To be honest with you though, by this time this chick had proved herself to be so mean, that I had lost all interest in sex anyway.

On arrival in Barcelona, we had problems getting the car on the Ferry. Getting uptight, Barbara left the car with me and booked herself as a passenger on the next boat. Miraculously, she put me in a hotel for the night. She fucking had to really, because if she hadn't, I would have just fucked off with her car. Having safely seen Barbara off on the ferry, I met up with some African guys, (total strangers) who sold me some smoke. It was all very friendly, and I drove them, in Barbara's new Volvo, to the beach to chill out and have a spliff or two. It was a quiet night, and thank God, the Volvo was in still in tact when I caught the ferry the following morning to Ibiza.

Barbara met me at the docks, and we drove the car to her place. It was at that point that the social problems between Barbara and myself arose.

At that time Franco was still in charge of Spain, and Ibiza was full of American ex-patriots, all of whom were only staying there with tourist visas. Once or twice Barbara had me drive some American friends of hers back over the border to France to get their passport stamped, so they could stay another six months. Barbara's friends felt that although my birth sign was a cool sign I wasn't somehow one of them. I was never completely relaxed in their company, and the vibes were never right. The whole crowd didn't seem to want me around. Barbara did not need me to drive the Volvo anymore, and now seemed to be totally ignoring me.

Instead of staying on with Barbara I began hanging out on the waterfront in Ibiza. Waterfronts were second home to me, anywhere and everywhere all over the world. One night in a bar I heard this guy speaking English with a Scottish accent. I went up to him and said, "Hey you're English." He said "English? Fuck off I'm Scottish!" We never became friends, but it was nice to have some one to talk to.

A day or so later, I met Jim, a student from Philadelphia, USA, and we became friends. Jim liked dope and with this vital habit in common we liked each other. Jim asked me if I wanted to go to a full moon party on the next island. I was broke, but Jim offered to pay for the ferry. Two hours later, we were both heading towards Furmeiteria, on a half-hour long boat ride.

On the island, we found the party in full swing, with two or three hundred people, all dancing in different groups, with alternative types of music.

Everyone was stoned, and the tequila was flowing. We all had a good time, and it was a wild party that went on all night. In those days, no party actually ever finished. My whole life was a party of one type or another.

A couple of days later, Jim suggested that I join him, and go to Morocco. Jim's reasoning was quite simple. He felt that he would be safer accompanied by me, a black guy, in Morocco.

In my heart I wanted to go back to England, but as per usual I got sucked into the flow of things, and my reply was, "Go to Africa? Yeah, why not?" One hour later we were on a boat to Valencia from where we hitchhiked all the way down to the coastline to where we caught the ferry to Morocco.

We docked and Jim desperate for a smoke bought some henna, which he stupidly thought was dope. Of course it wasn't, and he was ripped off. We then caught the bus to Tangiers and then on to Casablanca. No sooner had we got off the bus in Casablanca, than we realized that Jim's coat had gone missing along with his passport and travellers cheques.

In a panic, we first went to the American embassy, who directed us to report it to the local police station. Inside the police station, there was a white guy with dread locks behind a counter, smoking a keif pipe. The entire station had an aroma of peace and love, which was coming from his pipe. Seeing me staring at him in amazement, the guy actually made a gesture and offered me a drag on the pipe. The head policeman didn't take to kindly to this, and pushed this man, who apparently was a draft dodger, further back inside the station. Back at the embassy, after swearing his allegiance, they somehow gave Jim a new emergency passport.

A couple of weeks later, we met up with an English guy in Casablanca who had a Land Rover. Somehow, Jim and I did a deal with him to go back to England in his car. When we met in the YMCA in Casablanca, I was, as usual, chain smoking hash, and at first this English guy didn't want to be associated with me, and said that if we wanted a lift back to London I would have to cool it dope-wise, because they were smuggling back eight kilos. Eager to get the lift, I cooled it, smoked all my dope, and travelled back dope free. From Casablanca we went to Tangiers and then through Spain and France, to Calais. We drove through Calais with no problems, but at Dover, I knew it would get tricky. My name was still a bit hot at customs. I suggested to the guys that I would go through alone, and meet up with them later. I was searched, but the Land Rover got through with no problems, and we all met outside in the street. With us all laughing we then drove back to London. I was due a pay off from the smuggled dope and arranged to meet the guys in a few days time when they'd sold the dope. Sadly my pay off never came. The other passengers in the car were two girls, totally unaware that there was smuggling going on. I was told later that these honest girls had found out that there was dope in the Land Rover, and had threatened to tell the police. The guys got rid of the dope,

I got nothing out of it at all, and another episode of my life, like a spliff, got stubbed out.

CHAPTER 27
GETTING MARRIED

Life continued and I now settled down or at least lived in Blackheath in London. I had a new flat at 12 Lee Road. It had become an 'open house', for people in transit, that knew us. There was always a lot of smoke about, and the 'groovy' people passing through London, would know where to come to chill out and smoke a joint. The legend of 12 Lee Road was known all over the world. "Ask for Johnny, he'll role you one." Strangers would knock on our door, having been recommended to us by all sorts of people in Greece, or even as far away as America, knowing it was a cool place to be. The rules were simple. If the new face at the door could mention that they knew someone we trusted, they were allowed in.

12 Lee Road was a cool pad.

One day, there was a new type of visitor to 12 Lee Road. A very special person was to come into my life.

I was about to meet a new type of women. This was the first straight chick I had ever met in my entire life. She was a Viking Princess, a beautiful and creative woman from Denmark. This young lady was totally different from any other women I had ever encountered. She not only had a beautiful face and body, she also had something else - a brain between her ears!

Vibeke was eighteen years old. She was tall, with a lovely frame – a beautiful body. All of her clothes, which she made herself, were groovy way-out colours. She invented her own colours by dyeing different materials. Music-wise, she wouldn't just listen to my jazz. She had her own tastes like, the Beatles, Crosby Stills and Nash. This chick had a mind of her own. This girl really was so cool.

When I first saw Vibeke, I thought to myself, "There's a nice chick." She was very young, about eighteen years old. My philosophy then had always been that I would never do anything to anyone, that I wouldn't like to be done to me. For example, I wouldn't like some old bastard sleeping with my daughter when she was eighteen years old. I had strong principles. However my principles were tested to the limit one night, solely due to the lack of bed space.

Vibeke was sleeping alone in her bedroom in the flat, and it was about 12 o'clock at night.

Every other bed was full and I was tired, so tired in fact, that regardless of my principles, I was forced to get into bed with Vibeke was asleep as I climbed into her bed, but not wanting to disturb her, I kept as quiet as I could. A man has principles, and with absolutely no sexual thoughts whatsoever, well perhaps just a couple, I closed my eyes and went to sleep.

In the morning we did communicate however, in more ways than one. We fell in love there and then. A short while later, I had hardly got dressed before we were deciding to get married. It was all very quick and romantic. We really were so much in love.

Vibeke was so different from all the women I had ever met before. All my life, hookers, nightclub dancers, and hustlers had surrounded me. This woman was a revelation for me. She crotched her own cloth while I held the wool for her. She brought in her own loom, which took up half the room, and wove beautiful fabrics I had ever seen. For me she made Lee Road feel like home. I'd never had this feeling before in my life. It was beautiful. Vibeke did not smoke the weed at all, but she didn't disapprove of me smoking, because if you fell in love with Johnny, you had to take the weed with the man.

I had been a womaniser all my life. 'Love them and leave them and never go back', was my motto. I can only remember one time in my entire life when I actually did go back to a chick the day after - I had to. This chick greeted me and said,

"I knew you'd come back to me. You left your weed here last night."

With Vibeke though, it was so, so different. Not only did I go back, but also I wanted to go back - I was in love.

The wedding day soon arrived, and Vibeke's parents came over from Denmark for the wedding. Vibeke had crocheted her own wedding dress in white which looked amazing. Her wedding ring was made from beads, and that day she really looked like my own personal Viking Princess. It was all like a scene from a romantic Hollywood movie. We were married in Lewisham registry office. Our wedding guests were a very mixed bunch. We had: respectable relatives from Denmark; part-time weekend hippies; dropouts from Blackheath;

neighbours, and of course hardened dope smokers from my inner circle.

After we were married, we all went back to 12 Lee Road for our official wedding reception. Jim, my friend, had a load of credit cards, and did a sort-of runner at the local grocery store, getting crates and crates of champagne. He bought so much champagne, that he had to phone us from Sainsburys, to come and collect it all. The only transport we had was an old Baby Austin car, making it look very dodgy for Jim, buying all that champagne with dubious credit cards. Somehow, we managed to stuff all the booze in the car, and drive back to 12 Lee Road. Not sticking strictly to the wedding present list, of kettles and food mixers, one of my friends had given me the best wedding present of all: a half pound of the best quality Afghan hash.

There wc were, with thirty or forty guests crammed into our small flat together with crates of champagne and half a pound of Afghan smoke. My new wife's father, who was a dentist, was there along with a load of other straight people from Vibeke's side of the family. What we had to do was separate the wedding reception into two groups. The 'straights' were kept down stairs, sipping champagne and eating their cucumber sandwiches, while the 'in-crowd' were upstairs smoking their dope. Having only just got married, I obviously wanted to give a good impression to my new mother and father-in-law. To ensure peace and harmony I enrolled Vibeke's sister to make sure that her dad did not come upstairs while we were smoking our dope. There was a lot of action, with the 'in-crowd' going up and down the stairs to have a puff, before socialising with the 'straights' downstairs.

The wedding reception actually lasted for about a week, but the 'straights' left the following day. The dope was so intense that the 'in crowd' were spaced out all over the place, with half-smoked spliffs all over the floor. Everybody was happy, we all had a great time and I had married my Viking princess.

A year later Vibeke was pregnant, and at the time we were living in Ireland, near Waterford. It was a bad pregnancy and she was bleeding so much that we thought it better for her to go back and be in Denmark. There, the doctor advised that she should have an abortion. He explained that there were quite serious complications, and that if the child was born, it could be deformed, and that was our choice. Vibeke was heart broken. It was a hard decision, but we made it together and she had her abortion.

A year later God smiled on us and Vibeke was pregnant again. Yasmin was born in Denmark, and I was a Dad. The next part of my life was very confusing, and when I look back at it, it was very sad, but at the time I knew no better. Living in Denmark as a family was so strange for me because I had never had any experience of living as a proper family before. As a child, my father was a sailor, with a woman in every port and that's what I believed to be a normal.

A normal family life is being with your wife and kids, but I didn't know how to embrace this new deal. Nobody had ever shown me how to be a proper father and husband to my family. I tried, but sadly didn't try hard enough. Life, in its own chaotic way, carried on, and we moved back to England, Greenwich. My second daughter, Camilla, was born in Greenwich hospital. I regret it so much but sadly I wasn't there for her birth. The 'wonder-lust' had taken over and I was back in Morocco with a new chick called Jane.

In spite of my ways, miraculously Vibeke, Yasmin and Camilla still love me, although they think I'm one of the most irresponsible dads on earth.

Life continued.

Vibeke and I had been on one of our trips to Denmark, when more trouble had erupted. We had driven back and when we arrived at the boarder, there were problems bringing my car back in. Rather than delay my wife and daughter, I decided to let them go ahead, while I argued with customs. They made their own way back to London and went home.

Vibeke, being house-proud, started to clean up the flat. She made the bed and in the bed was one big problem. Vibeke found a pair of Jane's drawers under the sheets.

War broke out!

Later I confronted Jane who swore that she had not left her drawers there on purpose, but I didn't believe her.

The whole thing was a set-up. This was Jane at her conniving worst. Unaware of what was about to explode I finally got back to London and was greeted with:

" Where did these lace drawers come from?"

Caught red-handed, I took a deep puff on my spliff and came clean. I had no choice. I could hardly say the wind blew the drawers in through the window.

Vibeke was not very pleased to say the least. This was a very emotional time for all of us.

Looking back I was a motherfucker. I was a bastard. I wish I had done things differently. I now moved in to Jane's flat, but that wasn't so easy going. The next few years were totally intermingled and mish-mashed into each other, and probably loads of children, of which I was father to, were born all over London that I will never know about.

Vibeke moved back to Denmark in 1980, and Jane gave birth to Melody. On that first Christmas with Jane, I took her and Melody over to stay at Vibbika's in Denmark. I had a purpose. Jane now really wanted to set up a new life - a really proper life.

"New family life?" I said. "Fuck it. I've already got a family."

I told Jane that the only way I could have a family life with her would be to incorporate her into my existing family. I suppose part of my thinking was inherited from my father with his 'girl in every port' mentality.

After all, Melody was Yasmin's and Camilla's sister,

"Let's all live as one happy family, with peace and love," I said.

At first it all seemed to work out. Well, even the dentist father-in-law seemed to accept the new family set up, although he never did start smoking dope. At that time, I thought to myself, "What's the big deal? It's not everyday I bring another mother and child into the family. I've only done it once, and don't see any reason for anyone to get over upset."

Vibeke now lives permanently in Denmark. We got divorced and she has since got married to an American man called Hilton. He's a nice guy, and has brought the kids up well. They are all doing well. Regardless of my differences with Jane, what did come out of it was a wonderful daughter in Melody.

CHAPTER 28
JAZZ CLUBS

After Vibeke went to live in Denmark I started to concentrate on jazz clubs. It was my contribution to life - keeping music live. There is no substitution for a live musician. A Jazz musician is like a fine wine – the mellow with age.

I knew a guy called Mike Cantey, who offered me a venue in an old warehouse called Waterside, in Rotherhide. I was buzzing and very proud that I was now going to open my very own jazz club. I called my club 'The Edge'. The warehouse was a beautiful building that overlooked the river with big plate glass windows from which you could see Tower Bridge.

I now had a problem I had no   money to get booze into my new jazz club. I knew a lot of cool faces in those days and one of those was a guy called Paddy Onions. Paddy was a real old time gangster, from Blackheath. He took me to meet some Greek guys who owned an off-license in Bermondsey, and they supplied me with the booze on a sale or return basis. Alan, who ran the Crown Pub, in Blackheath, supplied me with beer on the same basis.

Another mate of mine called Bo made up some posters for me, Bo went on to be an expert poster designer. I never had a proper licence to sell the booze so I used to get a temporary licence via a pub called the New Concorde. This publican applied for an occasional licence, which I got for three-month periods.

My club was very popular, showcasing some of the biggest names on the jazz circuit: Django Bates, Harry Beckett, Stan Tracy, Barbara Thompson and Mike Osborne. Many well-known jazz musicians today were playing in my club at the beginning of their careers. Every club needs security bouncers on the door. Security costs money, but I came up with an idea to solve this one, I let in some of London's most notorious criminals for free. They were big spenders, who just wanted a place to drink, and if fights broke out they would be quick in regaining order. This way there was no hassle and the musicians were free to play until they were ready to stop often playing all through the night. The club got a lot of media attention. One evening newspaper described it as, "Quite the most atmospheric new jazz place in London." To add to the ambience of the venue there was plenty of dope about. It was this, my open-minded approach that made the club so popular. My club stayed open for a year.

'Edges', my jazz club was every Friday night and on Saturday nights the same venue was taken over by a rock 'n' roll promoter. He always allowed a group of about five or six guys to stay behind drinking late. One night they refused to leave and it all got out of hand. The bar maid wanted to close up shop but the guys wouldn't leave. She went to ring the police and one of the guys ripped the phone off the wall. Somehow she got herself out of the club but the guys, all the worse for ware with drink, barricaded themselves in and wrecked up the venue. One guy went around with a broom handle and smashed every glass in the place. This was a really wild mob and that was the end of my jazz club. People were still calling me years later asking when the famous jazz club would re-open.

Not so long after the closure a friend, whom I refer to as my adopted son, Osmond, who was very into jazz dancing, encouraged me to organise a national jazz dancing competition. I set up my own company, the 'Edge Music Organisation' to promote the evening. The competition was held at the Jazz Café, in Camden. It boasted Britain's top five jazz dancers performing in a live session with a one time only jazz quintet including Clifford Jarvis and Simon Picard.

This was the beginning of my new career as a successful jazz promoter and I continued in the industry for twenty years promoting live jazz, for venues like, 'The Creek' in Greenwich, the 'Greenwich Theatre' and 'Albany empire' to name but a few. I am and have always been a jazz- man and that's what makes me happy.

Regrets, I have got a few, and more than a few to mention. One is the way I treated my wife Vibeke. I wasn't a proper husband or father. Your house is only going to be as good as your foundation. Looking back now, if I had my time again, I would have done it all differently. I had my princess, a beautiful princess, and I lost her. In losing Vibeke I lost probably the most precious thing in my life. I am very proud of all my daughters and the way Vibeke brought them up. Today, Yasmin and Camilla are educated young women; Camilla is now a teacher of special needs children and Yasmin, inheriting her mother's creative side, designs and makes children's clothes. I also have got two wonderful grandchildren, Filippa and Kajsa. Melody is twenty-one years old with a life in front of her, and I am hopeful that she will give a good account of herself. Today Melody and I are the very best of friends and some days when Melody comes to visit me I see this stunning clever young woman full of life, and I think to myself, "Fuck man, that's my daughter, and I'm so proud of her." Here I am, sitting here aged sixty-nine, still smoking my dope and diggin' jazz. It's a long time since I got on that boat in Antigua. A lot of water has gone under the bridge, and a lot of dope has gone up in smoke. If I could get back all the money I have spent on dope, I'd be a millionaire. But fuck it, an old dog don't change his ways, and I'd rather be stoned than rich. The bell will toll for us all one day, and just in case God doesn't have a joint rolled for me in heaven, I will take one of my own up.

Thank you for reading my story.

EPILOGUE:

STEPHEN WARD: Stephen Ward died on August 3rd 1963 and with him went his espionage secrets. For many Stephen's death was a blessing because if he had been found guilty of living on immoral earnings and with nothing more to lose Stephen would have possibly exposed other high-ranking government officials who had collaborated with him in passing on secrets to the Russians.

JOHN PROFUMO: John devoted much of his life to working for Toynbee Hall and East London centre for alcoholics, drug addicts and dropouts. Initially he worked on a voluntary basis three days a week. Today he's 82 years old. In 1975 he was awarded the CBE for his charity work. His wife Valerie Hobson who had stood by him throughout sadly died in 1999. They have a son called David who is a writer.

EUGENE IVANOV: Prompted by Stephen Ward Ivanov left England in 1963 and returned to Moscow. He was suspended from the Communist Party due to the enquiry into his role in the Profumo scandal. His wife left him after hearing about his affair with Keeler. The last years of his life were quite sad. He lived alone and in January 1994 he drank himself to death and was found dead in his Moscow flat. He was 68 years old.

LORD DENNING: Denning lived in a large house in Hampshire. He left the court of appeal in 1982. He has been referred to as, 'The greatest judge of the century'. He died on the 6th March 1999. He was 100 years old.

LORD ASTOR: Astor died in 1966 at the height of the scandal. His wife claimed the Profumo case had caused her husband's death.

THE KRAY TWINS: The Krays were undisputedly the most feared gangsters of the entire era. Prepared to take violence to its extreme and murder when necessary they dominated people from all walks of life. As their empire spread from the East End of London to the fashionable Knightsbridge so did their involvement in all areas of corruption to the highest possible level. They were imprisoned in 1968. Ronnie Kray died on the 26th March 1995 and Reggie Kray died in October 2000.

HAROLD WILSON: Harold Wilson and his Labour government came to power on the 15th October 1964 and he remained party leader until 1976. Harold Wilson died with his own secrets on May 24th 1995.

HAROLD MACMILLAN: Macmillan was Prime Minister at the time of the Profumo affair. He resigned in October 1963. He finally retired from politics in October 1964, a casualty of the Keeler/Profumo saga. Sir Alec Douglas-Home took over as Prime Minister until Labour defeated them at the general election in 1964. He died in 1986.

MANDY RICE-DAVIES: After the Profumo scandal Mandy worked on the nightclub circuit, then married her first husband in Israel. She has appeared in plays both on stage and television as well as being a successful novelist. Now aged 57 and a grandmother she lives with her third husband, Ken Foreman. They own three homes in Miami, Bahamas and Surrey. Mandy was and has always been the most outspoken about the Profumo scandal.

CHRISTINE KEELER: Christine Keeler now lives in a flat in North London. She has two sons. In the year 2000 Christine wrote details of how she was manipulated by Stephen Ward in his acts of espionage.

JOHN EDGECOMBE TODAY

DOPE! A MESSAGE

Dope isn't what it used to be in Britain. I haven't been stoned, I mean really stoned, since the fifties and sixties. You cats out there who had been turning on for years would know what I am saying, and there was a lot more choice. Congo Matardi from the Belgian Congo, true brown from Rangoon, Tie Sticks, Afghan, Temple Balls. That is just to mention a few. But things were a lot different then. Smuggling was easy and there were lots of smugglers. Most of them were smokers and didn't want to bring anything back that they wouldn't smoke themselves and if they manage to bring back fifty kilos, that was a big deal. There was only one Howard Marks then, so the man was more concerned with stamping on the demand. They were so eager to bust the smokers that if a man was murdering his wife and some guys next door were having a party and smoking dope and if they couldn't deal with both at the same time, I think that they would raid the party first. Naturally, in the old days most of the consumers were black. It was easier to get busted for possession than smuggling.

I had never smuggled. It's not that I wasn't tempted, only I knew that the odds were stacked against me. Being a guy who is black and infamous, I knew that I would never get passed the customs. I never have without being confronted by them. But it was cool for the cats that were white. Some of them used to do it alone. All they needed was two passports and a holiday in France. If you had a sidekick who was bringing the stuff into France it would be just a day trip. The black cats had their own way of dealing with it, without going through customs. The Indians were a major source of supply. They were sailors on British ships, working for slave wages, and needed to supplement it. If you can dig that four Indians wages only amounted to that of one English sailor, then you would agree a supplement was in order. Not to mention the producer, the banana ganja boat.

Back then we were a kind of society. I met most of my friends through dope, and we are still friends. We knew that getting high was cool and forever will be. Dope is the safest drug known to us. You can't OD on it. But easy on the tobacco. That's the only danger in smoking dope. Still governments talk about alcohol abuse and banning tobacco advertising. But that's just part of their psychology, to increase the treasury funds. You can't abuse alcohol, or anything else without abusing yourselves. Well! There are millions of us who don't want to abuse ourselves with alcohol and we want to talk about dope and democracy. We know that the main reasons why we are being criminalized for our choice of drug are purely economic and not out of any concern for our health. It's part of their protection racket. They won't legalize it until they can figure out how to control the revenue and that isn't going to be easy. They will have a lot of figuring out to do, like, how will it affect their revenue on the alcohol trade, which is already suffering from reasonably priced, illegal import.

We know that we are dealing with dogmatic hypocrites, and some of them, at the moment, as I am writing, are probably smoking a real nice spliff from dope they smuggled in their diplomatic bag. Like their predecessors, they aren't going to give, unless we force them. We are going to have to raise the stakes and start lighting up in public places where smoking is allowed. Demand our rights. Cannabis is God's gift to us. You don't have to make it, just grow it and smoke it. Governments have no democratic right to make it illegal for any one to grow a plant, unless the plant is dangerous. Can you dig it? If you are drunk and just ran over some one and killed them you still have a case of whiskey in your boot, but the cops can't confiscate it. They don't dig us being in control of ourselves. They want us to stick to the pub culture, get pissed, make assas of ourselves, which, if we remember, the next day, we will try to forget; and if you didn't wake up in jail and have to pay some more tax, you could call yourself lucky. I know, I've been there. Under booze control. Remember the Red Indians. They called it firewater and it played a major part in wasting them while the white man ripped off the land. Most of the crimes committed in our society are booze related and the system makes allowances for the extent of your condition. They accept the fact that booze is bad news; at the same time denying us our rights to smoke dope, in the face of strong public opinion, in favour of legalizing it. What kind of democracy are we talking about here?

Well, I am a Jazzman. I love it, and dope enhances all the things I dig, chills my anxiety and explores my imagination. I am not about to stop.

SEASONED DOPE SMOKER AGED 40

ME ON THE HIGH SEAS & IN ROME AGED 36

LUCKY GORDON & MYSELF BEING
TAKEN FROM WANDSWORTH PRISON TO
VISIT LORD DENNING

VIBEKE MY EX-WIFE

YASMIN AGED 30

CAMILLA AGED 28

BROKEN
JUSTICE

A LETTER TO THE READERS FROM MELODY JOHNS DAUGHTER

My Dad is the kindest, nicest man I know. He's pukka. When I was fourteen my mother abandoned me. My Dad rescued me. Suffering from depression for ages I just sat in his armchair with tears streaming down my face. My Dad looked after me and always tried to make me feel happier and in the end I did. He gave me lifts to and from school everyday, and even when I went to college, but I know he didn't mind because it was for my education. He didn't bother going to school himself much and I think he wishes he had.

My Dads sweet like I can go round there anytime, plot for a little while, have a smoke and a giggle with him. My friends all love him. Boyfriends though are either petrified or in awe of him but he's a real softie really. I do worry about him a lot though 'cause he's nearly seventy and goes on like he's still in his twenties taking E's and beeping at birds with big boobs! But that's him all over, he's a geezer. I can't imagine how hard his life has been. I admire him. I love my Dad more than anything.

ME & MY DAUGHTER MELODY

THANK YOU

Thanks to the following people without whose help
this book would not be possible.

Melody, James Wilson, Kirsten Short, Greg Bennett,
Bob Powell, Mark Badger, Valerie Giral,
Claudia Ward, Paul Smith, Simon May,
Tania Oliver and Julian.

And of course the dope dealers whose wonderful
products kept my mind alive whilst writing.

"Decade of love
Decade of the flower
Decade for youth
Decade of power"

The 60's was a time of peace and love
Dressed so swish, fab music and as high as a dove
Smoke filled rooms, the sound of a heavy beat
Life was perfect from beneath your sheet

Far away from those Caribbean days
Where the lights of London turned reality to a haze
Sucked into a world so sinister and new
I lived, I thrived on what I had to do

Relive with me those crazy days
Close your eyes and envisage the scene
Of a time of intrigue, a time of scandal
Where life was not always the dream

A poem for Johnny by Claudia Maria Ward April 2002

AN INCREDIBLE TRUE STORY

NOTTING HILL GIRL

At the age of ten I was addicted to weed, heroin, and cocaine. I did it all. My nightmare twenty-year horror trip took me into the violent yardie gangster world, the darker side of Notting Hill Gate.

I saw crack cocaine arrive and change the peace and love drug scene into hell on earth.

Crack cocaine spread from the ghetto to the rich and poor suburbs and is now in every school playground in England.

My story reflects life in every city today and I hope by reading it others still out there can see there is a better life if they want it.

Notting Hill Girl out now in paperback £6.99
ISBN 0-9529215-4-5

NOTTING HILL
GIRL

The incredible true story of a thirteen year old trapped in London's drug web

"It's a miracle I survived to tell it all"

Denise Watson

edited by Roy Ward Baker

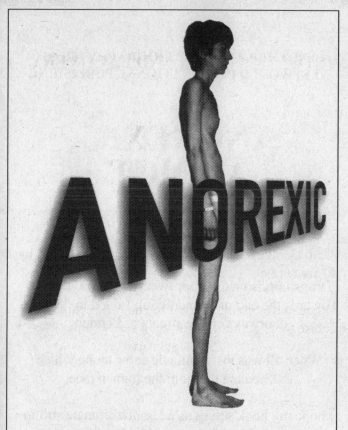

ANOREXIC

THE INCREDIBLE TRUE STORY OF A YOUNG GIRL'S JOURNEY TO HELL AND BACK

IT'S A MIRACLE I FOUND LOVE AND
LIVED TO WRITE THIS BOOK

ANNA PATERSON

**ANOTHER AMAZING BIOGRAPHY FROM
WESTWORLD INTERNATIONAL PUBLISHING**

ADDICT

A true story by Stephen Smith

Drugs imprisoned me for twenty years of my life.
Towards the end of my addiction I lived in the shop
doorways on the streets of London.

When all was lost a miracle came along which
enabled me to rejoin the human race.

I hope my book serves as a lesson fortunate still in
the clutches of addiction.

**Addict out now in paperback in all book shops £6.99
ISBN 0-9529215-0-2**

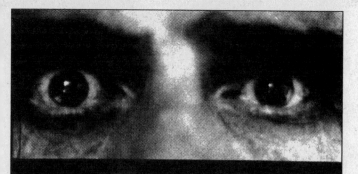

ADDICT

AN INCREDIBLE TRUE STORY WITH A FAIRYTALE END

A TWENTY-YEAR DRUG AND DRINK HORROR TRIP FROM RICHES TO INSANITY IN THE GUTTER

STEPHEN SMITH